School Safety

School Safety

True Stories and Solutions from School Leaders

Edited by Rocky Wallace, Stephanie Sullivan, and Ann Burns

ROWMAN & LITTLEFIELD
Lanham • Boulder • New York • London

Published by Rowman & Littlefield
An imprint of The Rowman & Littlefield Publishing Group, Inc.
4501 Forbes Boulevard, Suite 200, Lanham, Maryland 20706
www.rowman.com

86-90 Paul Street, London EC2A 4NE

Copyright © 2024 by Rocky Wallace

All rights reserved. No part of this book may be reproduced in any form or by any electronic or mechanical means, including information storage and retrieval systems, without written permission from the publisher, except by a reviewer who may quote passages in a review.

British Library Cataloguing in Publication Information Available

Library of Congress Cataloging-in-Publication Data

Names: Wallace, Rocky, 1956- editor. | Sullivan, Stephanie (Stephanie Dawn), editor. | Burns, Ann, (Ann H.), editor.
Title: School safety : true stories and solutions from school leaders / edited by Rocky Wallace, Stephanie Sullivan and Ann Burns.
Other titles: School safety (Rowman and Littlefield, Inc.)
Description: Lanham, MD : Rowman & Littlefield, [2024] | Includes bibliographical references.
Identifiers: LCCN 2023056675 (print) | LCCN 2023056676 (ebook) | ISBN 9781475871562 (cloth) | ISBN 9781475871579 (paperback) | ISBN 9781475871586 (ebook)
Subjects: LCSH: Schools--Safety measures. | School violence--Prevention.
Classification: LCC LB2864.5 .S369 2024 (print) | LCC LB2864.5 (ebook) | DDC 371.7--dc23/eng/20231218
LC record available at https://lccn.loc.gov/2023056675
LC ebook record available at https://lccn.loc.gov/2023056676

Contents

Foreword	vii
Acknowledgments	ix
Introduction *Byron Darnall and Lu Settles Young*	1
Chapter 1: Missing Child *Rocky Wallace*	9
Chapter 2: One Down . . . Maybe More *Stephanie Sullivan and Abbigail Morris*	13
Chapter 3: Panic at the Disco *Ann Burns*	23
Chapter 4: Phrases *Keith Griesser*	27
Chapter 5: Community Disaster *Abbigail Morris*	33
Chapter 6: Not in My School *Chuck Hamilton*	39
Chapter 7: We Have a Runner *Neely Traylor*	47
Chapter 8: The Apple Did Not Fall Far from the Tree *William Ingle*	51
Chapter 9: Kentucky Office of the State School Security Marshal: School Safety and Resiliency Act of 2019 *Ben Wilcox*	55

Chapter 10: Fear of the Unknown — 59
Brett Burton

Chapter 11: Enraged Student — 67
Veda Stewart

Chapter 12: The Power of a Trusting Relationship — 71
Carrie Ballinger

Chapter 13: Leadership Practices for Success in Crisis Situations — 75
Kevin Hub

Chapter 14: Keep Everyone Safe — 81
Michael W. Kessinger

Chapter 15: Baby Bear Wants His Porridge . . . Now! — 91
Franklin Thomas

Chapter 16: Bad Decisions Can Be Made with the Best of Intentions — 95
Rebecca Howell

Chapter 17: Ready at All Costs or Ready at All? — 99
Leslie Todd Watts

Chapter 18: We Can't Do Everything — 105
Krystal Conway-Cunningham and Michael W. Kessinger

Chapter 19: The Quiet Kid — 109
Taylor Lauck and Christina Drury

Chapter 20: Anonymous Caller — 113
J. P. Rader

Chapter 21: It's Not Going to Happen Here — 117
Bill Sullivan

Chapter 22: Cell Phone Safety — 123
Myram Brady, Rachel Addison-Miller, and Pamela Puryear

Chapter 23: Security Scare Internet Style — 129
Holly Hunt and Kim Puckett

Chapter 24: Student Voice — 133
Toni Konz Tatman

Closing Thoughts — 139

Works Cited — 141

About the Editors — 147

Foreword

This compilation of true stories is a diverse mix of examples of the daily life inside a twenty-first-century school in the United States. Each author contributes an invaluable experience that is not only interesting to read but also challenging by providing clues on how to lead and grow healthier schools—physically, mentally, emotionally, and relationally; a culture of care.

From bullying to severe storms, from inappropriate relationships to alcohol abuse, from school shootings to kids "missing in action," this edited collection covers the gambit—and does so with doable solutions.

Some of the "lessons learned," that hopefully can be of assistance to our fellow educators and their schools, will be the following:

- Do you want students to be in the right places, at the right times, doing the right things?
- Assigning staff throughout the campus, actively engaged with students whether or not they are in class, is a huge part of the answer.
- Students and their emotional needs: Ignore them, and it is only a matter of time.
- Staff/student "out of bounds" relationships in your school district? No way! Right? Are you really that naive?
- Kids bullying kids. That was in years gone by, right? Actually, today, student-to-student harassment is more sophisticated and crueler than ever.
- Parents overprotecting their children when alcohol is involved? You betcha. And sometimes, they are the source!
- Do we really need all of those severe storm drills? Yes!
- School shootings . . . In my community? Yes.

If reading this book makes your school even safer in one area of the larger domain of "safe schools," then it will be more than worth it, and you will have played an important role while you take your turn as the gatekeeper—providing a safe haven for the precious children entrusted to your care.

Acknowledgments

The wisdom shared in this compilation of true stories on school safety is an amazing example of the caliber of leadership we have in our P–12 schools. Thanks to all contributors for reflecting on a time in their career as a school leader when a volatile situation was brewing and sharing how they calmly guided students and staff through choppy waters.

Special thanks to Jon Akers, executive director of the Kentucky Center for School Safety, for his invaluable contribution to schools regionally and across the nation.

Introduction

Byron Darnall and Lu Settles Young

OFFICE OF EDUCATOR LICENSURE & EFFECTIVENESS

Every school leader harbors one distinct fear . . . tragedy striking the school community.

Unfortunately, current reality suggests that all school leaders will encounter issues with school safety—either real or perceived. Aside from being an instructional leader, school manager, and inspirer, the school leader must also remain alert to any potential psychological or physical threats.

School safety goes beyond physically securing a building; it involves an iterative process of examining the culture and climate to ensure every human being that interacts with the school feels a sense of belonging and trust. Even when a school leader places a premium on fostering belonging, it remains a matter of time before a situation arises to challenge a school's safety.

Protecting students' well-being and earning custodial trust requires hypervigilance. Every day the school leader must read the building, read the students as they enter or pass in the hallway, read the teachers and administrators as they welcome students for the day, read the parents/guardians that drop off their child, and read the support staff and their interactions with students and staff. So much of protecting a school's safety comes down to observation and intuition, much of which is difficult to learn through preparation programs.

Even under the most prepared of circumstances, something unexpected will emerge. For example, a high school student will Airdrop a picture during lunch. Anyone nearby will receive the notification. A student across the cafeteria will accept the image. The image reveals another student appearing to hold a handgun. The recipient will panic, share it with friends via text and social media. Within seconds, the buzz begins to crescendo across the cafeteria, then through the school; soon, the phone calls begin.

Some may think elementary school to be less challenging, but again, it is only a matter of time before this assumption is challenged. For example, a student's father shows up to have lunch with his child. The father isn't recognized by the secretary; however, he is listed in the information management system and presents a corroborating piece of identification. The secretary has the wherewithal to notify the principal, and out of caution, the principal contacts the child's mother who has been involved with the school.

In shock, the mother lets the principal know the child has not seen the father in over six years because he was incarcerated. The principal asks the mother if the father's rights have been terminated, to which the mother responds, "No." Legally, the father has parental rights, but now the principal can only imagine the shock on the young student's face of seeing her father show up at school after a six-year absence.

One of the great aspects of being an elementary principal is observing or playing with students during recess. Even this becomes less safe when a car pulls up to the school yard fence and a male gets out of the vehicle, only to expose himself to nearby students and then quickly drive away. With a heavy heart, the principal composes a message for parents and guardians explaining the occurrence. The counselor and principal must also support the students that witnessed the inappropriate act and further communicate with their parents. This further complicates protecting the students' rights to recess while worrying if something like this might happen again.

Being a committed and caring school leader comes with near impossible expectations at times. School leaders, like everyone else in the school community, are human beings with limited capacity to imagine and prevent the myriad scenarios that may pose a threat. On the contrary, school leaders often receive the greatest criticism when something unfortunate occurs, and with this comes significant stress and concern.

No school leader ever wants to be saddled with something devastating. Nonetheless, it happens daily across the nation, and the general public rarely learns of what goes on behind the scenes before, during, or after any event. They do not see the silent moments in the office when the gravity of the situation hits. They do not see the emotional and physical toll it takes. They do not experience the sleepless nights or the brain that will not turn off.

The pages that follow offer sage advice from experienced school leaders. We learn most from our peers and consider this yet another network full of wisdom upon which to draw. Be grateful that the authors represented here care enough to share their stories, so that others might be better equipped when a situation arises. Everyone improves when they have trusted advisors. Friends, mentors, and colleagues must be a part of the school leaders' quiver to maintain, and most importantly, grow in their leadership.

Just like day one as the teacher of record in a classroom, no one steps into a school leadership role with any true sense of what is about to unfold. Yet, one also cannot fathom the rewards that come with being a school leader. The role, while grueling, offers one a unique window into so many moving interactions and so many lives. Despite all the things one cannot know, please know this: it is worth it!

THE RESEARCH: SAFE FROM THE INSIDE OUT

"There is not just a need for happier schools, schools where the children are free to do as they like or schools where they use certain materials: education today needs reform. If education is to prepare man for the present, and the immediate future, he will need a new orientation towards the environment."

—Maria Montessori

One of many residual effects of the COVID-19 pandemic on public education will most surely be the renaissance of the *whole child movement*, popularized in the United States by leading cognitive scientists and educators like John Dewey and Maria Montessori from the first half of the twentieth century. Teaching and nurturing the *whole child* recognizes the importance of developing the full spectrum of social, emotional, cultural, and cognitive abilities in learners, and it is through this lens that readers may find it beneficial to examine the complexity of school safety in twenty-first-century America.

This book is full of stories and real-world examples of leaders who can be characterized as school-safety heroes. Before we recount those stories, it is important to build a foundation around what we mean by school safety. In the context of the whole child movement in education, ASCD describes five tenets that are critical for children and youth to feel if we are to ensure their long-term development and success: healthy, safe, engaged, supported, and challenged (Whole Child Framework, 2023).

Within the context of a whole child framework, school safety means much more than securing buildings and grounds, deploying law enforcement agents in schools, and conducting active shooter training. While such security measures are essential in today's world, school safety must also account for keeping schools safe *from the inside out*. Every student has the right to a safe learning environment free from bullying and threats, in spaces where they feel emotionally and physically safe, and to experience a sense of belonging. To accomplish that sense of physical and emotional well-being, school leaders must expand their thinking to include human-centered responses to better meet the safety needs of students and adults.

SCHOOL SAFETY FROM THE INSIDE OUT

During a recent interview with Jon Akers, director of the Kentucky Center for School Safety, Mr. Akers talked about two key human capital resources that are essential in today's schools (J. Akers, personal communication, April 2023). He said that all schools need school safety personnel, including school resource officers, who have the skills and tactical equipment and training to keep schools secure from outside threats. Akers was equally adamant about the need for all schools to have mental health providers who tend to the needs of students and adults inside schools—including the need to be emotionally safe for themselves and others while developing a healthy sense of well-being.

Speaking directly to the mental health needs of students, Thomas Armstrong writes, "Mental health interventions are designed to improve the *internal* psychological world of students, so they are less apt to engage in violence and better able to handle the stress that accompanies incidents of trauma." Armstrong goes on to describe those interventions as "self-regulation strategies, like developing a growth mindset, creating better nutrition habits, engaging in physical exercise, and participating in emotional-intelligence activities that help students identify their moment-to-moment emotional states and establish ways to safely manage feelings when they are at or near the boiling point" (Armstrong 2019).

The work of Dan Olweus may also be of interest to the readers of this book as it relates to school safety from the inside out. Olweus (2013), who is renowned for his bullying prevention program, defined bullying as a kind of aggressive behavior intended to inflict harm on another (p. 756). He noted that bullying can be characterized by three criteria: intentionality, repetitiveness, and an imbalance of power. According to the US government's website, stopbullying.gov, about 20 percent of American students ages 12–18 have experienced bullying, and 19 percent of students in grades 9–12 reported being bullied on school property in the 12 months prior to the survey—and those numbers may be very low given that bullying often goes unreported (Assistant Secretary for Public Affairs [ASPA], 2021).

With the proliferation of student use of social media platforms, bullying that occurs in today's schools and communities is often characterized as *cyberbullying*, where bullies post or send harmful content about their victims with the intent to cause embarrassment or humiliation.

School leaders who are committed to school safety across the country are taking affirmative steps to eradicate all forms of bullying in their schools, often in partnership with local law enforcement officials. But such work is time-consuming and relentless. School safety teams are redoubling their efforts to re-norm their school cultures to increase reporting and provide targeted interventions to change the behaviors of bullies—while addressing the victimization and trauma experienced by students who have experienced bullying. These concerted efforts are another powerful example of building a safe school environment for all students and keeping schools safe from the inside out.

ENGAGING STUDENTS AS SCHOOL SAFETY THOUGHT PARTNERS

When considering how to keep schools safe from the inside out, the most important voice school leaders must amplify is that of students. In recent years, organized student-voice coalitions have proliferated across the United States. In Kentucky, the Prichard Committee for Academic Excellence established a student voice team in 2012 that became the independent, student-led Kentucky Student Voice Team (KSVT) in 2021.

This dynamic group of students from across the commonwealth mobilized an effort centered around school safety in 2018, following school shootings in Marshall County, Kentucky, and Parkland, Florida. In 2019, KSVT published *[S]he Matters: Peer-to-Peer Sexual Harassment in High School,* the report of a student-led research study conducted in partnership with [S]he Matters. This qualitative look at sexual harassment in schools relied on students hearing from other students about their lived experiences in schools. The report offered wide-ranging, student-oriented solutions—including more training and information about sexual harassment, dating violence, assault, revised dress code language, and avenues for confidential reporting and support.

In 2020, KSVT published *Coping with COVID-19 Student-to-Student Study*—designed to "understand Kentucky students' social-emotional and learning experiences during the first few months of the COVID-19 crisis" (2020, p.1). KSVT relied on the voices of students to shed light on the experiences real students have in real situations—in and out of school.

Among the many recommendations from the *Coping with COVID-19* study (2020) were several related to mental health, including ensuring mental health services are available to students, increasing the number of counselors in schools, providing training for teachers on social-emotional learning, and, in keeping with the theme of this chapter, the recommendation to "encourage social connection within and outside the regular curriculum and build a positive school climate for students to process" (p. 3).

Another active student voice group concerned about school safety is the Kentucky Department of Education's Commissioner's Student Advisory Council (SAC). This group of high school students, representing every geographical area of the state, released its own report in January 2023, called *A Focus on School Safety*. These students selected this topic in the aftermath of the school shooting in Uvalde, Texas, and devoted personal and collective time to develop a set of ten recommendations for schools.

Several of the recommendations implicated prevention efforts, including promoting the use of tip lines, improving behavior interventions, and supporting gun control legislation. To better support students and adults who encounter school violence, the Student Advisory Council recommended improved training and notification systems. The SAC concluded their report by reiterating the need for mental health support for students and adults, including access to therapy after a traumatic event.

The significance of these student-initiated efforts stems from the common themes found across the studies and the critical importance of hearing directly from students about issues of school safety and security—issues that directly affect their day-to-day lives. Joud Dahleh, one of the SAC study authors and student member of the Kentucky Board of Education, summed it up in an interview with the *Kentucky Teacher* (2023) when she said, "Our main goal is to make sure that everyone is getting a quality education and you cannot have a quality education if you do not feel safe in your school building (p. 1)." (See chapter 24 for more details on SAC's work.)

THE NEXUS BETWEEN SCHOOL SAFETY AND STUDENT ACHIEVEMENT

Most people would agree that the highest priority of schools is student learning, but also know that learning does not occur in a vacuum. There are a variety of factors that influence student achievement in schools, such as attendance, assessment, and a sense of well-being while at school (Kutsyuruba et al., 2015). School leaders play a key role in building schools that have safe, supportive cultures in which students thrive and learn, and this gold standard happens "by establishing, maintaining, sustaining, and brokering trust relationships in schools" (Kutsyuruba et al., 2015).

The importance of trust in schools cannot be overstated, and that trust must occur among all stakeholders—leaders, students, faculty, staff, families, and the larger community. Families choose to send their children to school every day. Whether they drop them off at the door or wave goodbye to them as they climb onto the school bus, they must draw from a well of trust in the system and in the individuals (drivers, teachers, monitors, cafeteria workers, administrators).

According to Gallup (Brenan, 2022), in August 2022, 44 percent of parent-respondents expressed fear for the safety of their children at school, second only to the 55 percent all-time high in 1999 shortly after 13 people were killed at Columbine High School in Littleton, Colorado. One in five parents in the same poll indicated that their children had expressed worry about school safety.

One of the fundamental research studies taught in school leadership preparation programs is Maslow's Hierarchy of Needs (1943). The hierarchy is depicted as a pyramid where the most basic level of need is physiological—the need for food, sleep, clothing, and shelter. Educators learn early on that children and youth who come to school hungry need to eat before they are able to learn. The next level of Maslow's Hierarchy is safety—the need for personal security. Unless schools are able to ensure students feel physically and emotionally safe at school, students will struggle to learn.

The renaissance of the whole child movement reminds us of Maslow's theory—that the full spectrum of student needs must be met if they are to learn and thrive in school. Feeling a sense of safety and belonging is not just nice, warm, and fuzzy; instead, school safety is fundamental to student achievement and therefore demands the time, attention, resources, and commitment of school leaders everywhere to keep their schools safe from the inside out.

REFERENCES

Advisory Groups—Kentucky Department of Education. (n.d.). Retrieved April 23, 2023, from https://education.ky.gov/CommOfEd/adv/Pages/default.aspx

Armstrong, T. (2019). School safety starts from within. *Educational Leadership*, 77(2), 48–52.

ASCD. (n.d.). *The whole child approach to education*. ASCD. Retrieved April 23, 2023, from https://www.ascd.org/whole-child

Assistant Secretary for Public Affairs (ASPA). (2021, September 9). *Facts about bullying*. StopBullying.gov. Retrieved April 23, 2023, from https://www.stopbullying.gov/resources/facts#_Fast_Facts

Brenan, M. (2022, December 6). *Parent, student school safety concerns elevated*. Gallup.com. Retrieved April 23, 2023, from https://news.gallup.com/poll/399680/parent-studentschoolsafety-concerns-elevated.aspx

Kentucky Student Voice Team. (2021). *Coping with COVID-19 student-to-student study*. 2nd ed. Retrieved April 23, 2023, from https://globaluploads.webflow.com/630e58db6406d5a8f8a3ab90/6323b53b768816703e06a9ed_Coping%20With%20COVID-19%20Executive%20Summary.pdf

KDE's Commissioner's Student Advisory Council Presents Recommendations to Increase School Safety. Kentucky Teacher. (2023, February 3). Retrieved April 23, 2023, from https://www.kentuckyteacher.org/news/2023/01/kdes-commissioners-student-advisory-council-presents-recommendations-to-increase-school-safety/

Kutsyuruba, B., Klinger, D. A., & Hussain, A. (2015). Relationships among school climate, school safety, and student achievement and well-being: a review of the literature. *Review of Education, 3*(2), 103–35

Maslow, A. H. (1943). A theory of human motivation. *Psychological Review,* 50(4), 370–96. doi: 10.1037/h0054346

Olweus, D. (2013). School Bullying: Development and Some Important Challenges. *Annual Review of Clinical Psychology, 9*(1), 751–80

Research. (S)HE Matters. (n.d.). Retrieved April 23, 2023, from https://shemattersky.org/research

School safety starts from within. ASCD. (n.d.). Retrieved April 23, 2023, from http://www.ascd.org/el/articles/school-safety-starts-from-within

Chapter 1

Missing Child

Rocky Wallace

In the back of a school leader's mind, it is noted that any day with students in the building can change in an instant. A "not on my watch" determination to prevent harm to students or the school can make all the difference.

John looked up from his desk just in time to see an obviously upset parent coming through his office door with her young son.

"Hello, Ma'am. How can I help you today?"

The mother appeared frazzled and was wild eyed. "How about you all paying more attention around here? Guess who walked in my front door about 15 minutes ago?"

She looked down at her little Cade—a second grader who had that expression on his face that made it obvious he knew he was in big trouble. "He walked right off your school's property, across main street in heavy traffic, down a few blocks, then across the railroad tracks. I can't imagine how he even made it home safely."

John was a veteran principal, but this was the first time he had experienced this particular crisis—a student leaving the school premises unsupervised and walking home. Before he could begin to settle Cade's mom down, she demanded that his homeroom teacher be called to the office.

"Yes, Mrs. Stone needs to be in this conversation. She's at lunch right now, I believe. I'll have my secretary call her." John wondered how Cade had gotten out of sight of one of the school's most experienced and dedicated teachers.

"I'll go straight to the school board over this. There is no excuse for such carelessness. Good grief! He could have been killed!" Cade looked up at his mother and began to cry. John made sure to keep the conversation calm and real, not defensive or trying to shift the blame.

Soon, Mrs. Stone appeared, pale-faced and visibly on edge.

"Why, hello Mrs. Parker. Oh, thank goodness! We've been looking all over our wing of the building for Cade! Cade, honey, where did you go? Why did you not go to lunch with your classmates? What is going on?"

"I'll tell you what's going on. You, or someone, didn't pay attention a few minutes ago, and Cade here decided to hike home. Little fella could have been the victim of a tragedy! Who dropped the ball on this, Mrs. Stone? My son is only seven years old!"

"Well, uh, looks like Cade broke one of our main rules and didn't follow directions in staying in line while leaving our room and going to lunch. He must have darted for the side door to the playground while we were traveling from the classroom to the cafeteria." The teacher, nearing the last chapter of her career, had been a colleague of John's since his first year of teaching. She looked at him, pleading for validation that this was the boy's fault—not hers.

Instead, John immediately took the conversation in an entirely different direction. "Mrs. Parker, I apologize for the school that this has happened. We have a strong, caring, dedicated staff here, and our routines are always about what's best for the kids—or we do our best to keep it that way. But obviously, something went wrong here. We'll take a close look internally, and whatever we need to do about our lunch protocols we will do it."

Mrs. Stone glared at John as if she could scold him right then and there in front of the little boy and his momma. But she was pale as a ghost and cotton mouthed when she tried to talk, so she remained silent.

John emphasized humility again. "I am sorry, Mrs. Parker. I can't imagine what trauma this has caused you."

"Well, I'll be at the next school board meeting," barked Mrs. Parker as she turned toward the door. The conversation was over. It may have lasted ten minutes or less. Mrs. Stone took

Cade back to lunch, Cade's mom went home, and John called the superintendent and filled him in on what had happened. Then he sat back in his chair, stared out the window, and prepared himself to read about the incident in the local paper the next day.

John knew if it made it to the local news office—even though the reporters there had been a friend to him and the school over the years—they would not kill the story. They couldn't.

Keeping it under wraps would be considered negligence in the world of news reporting and holding public agencies accountable.

But the next day came, and no story. It was not in the local paper and not on local TV. John was relieved but knew it was probably coming at the next board meeting. And sure enough, when that evening rolled around, there was

Mrs. Parker—sitting in the back of the audience. It just so happened that this month's meeting had been scheduled for John's school, and some of the school's strengths were featured.

The agenda rolled along, and finally the board chair adjourned the session. Mrs. Parker sat silent the whole time, not saying a word. And from that day forward she never did mention the incident again. Neither did Mrs. Stone.

Over the years, John has often looked back to that moment in time, when an ordinary school day suddenly turned into an extraordinary, volatile, "what have we gotten ourselves into here" situation—in an instant. Today, over two decades later, he shares the event with his grad students, who are preparing to be school leaders. John, his teacher, his school, and district could have so easily been sued. They would have lost if the parent's grievance did go to litigation.

What kept Mrs. Parker from following through with her intent to pursue further avenues by taking the matter to the school board?
John cannot explain it for sure. However, he has always felt the sincere, authentic apology—from the heart—helped Mrs. Parker to find grace on her son's school; grace that maybe she did not even know she had.

Jon Akers, the director of the Kentucky Center for School Safety, says that "One of the more effective strategies school officials can implement in order to prevent harm to students is to have adults intentionally and consistently assigned throughout the building. By engaging in 'active supervision' practices, whereby the staff member roves in an assigned zone/area, constantly greeting/chatting with students, as opposed to 'passive supervision,' where the staff member does not engage/talk with students and remains static in one place not moving, it makes a huge difference."

Akers adds this: "This same 'active supervision' strategy can easily be applied to include lunch supervision, class changes, when students are arriving and/or during dismissal, bathroom breaks, back hallways, and when students transition throughout all remote portions of the school building. The key here is continuous engagement with students and not remaining in one place. A drawback with 'passive supervision' practices is that students will be able to quickly determine areas where staff members are *not* supervising and will start to gather in the unattended areas of the school building."

CHAPTER SUMMARY

An experienced principal and an experienced classroom teacher find themselves on the verge of litigation—without much hope of not being found negligent. Yet, partly due to the principal's attitude of remorse and sincere apology, instead of being defensive and overprotective, a concerned mother seems to forgive and models grace in return.

QUESTIONS FOR REFLECTION

1. Can you think of a time when you as an educator (or your school) were vulnerable due to allowing a student or students to find themselves in a dangerous situation?
2. Does your school check safety protocols regularly, looking for weaknesses in the day-to-day processes?
3. If you had been in John's shoes, how might you have handled the situation differently?

REFERENCE

Akers, J. (2023). Kentucky Center for School Safety. Richmond.

Chapter 2

One Down ... Maybe More

Stephanie Sullivan and Abbigail Morris

It was school spirit day, and students were gathering in the commons, waiting for the bell to ring to be dismissed to class. All of a sudden, there was a loud noise that sounded like balloons popping or fireworks exploding. Was this something related to spirit day? People began running ... but why?

Superintendent Smith

6:15 a.m.

As Mr. Smith waited for his daughter to get ready for school, he sat at his kitchen table scrolling through Twitter, pleased to be retweeting a positive message about the school district. He took a few more minutes to type, "We know we have great teachers in our region," as he linked an article highlighting the gains teachers make with students who come to school well below grade level. "What a great way to start the day!" he thought. Ready to leave for work, he looked at the time and called to his daughter, a freshman at the local high school. "It is time for school."

Joining the long line of parents waiting to drop off their children, Superintendent Smith watched as the teachers greeted the students, waved to the parents and sometimes shared a few words before driving away. Finally reaching the drop-off area, his daughter said a quick "I love you, Dad" before turning to join some friends and hurry into school.

Driving a short distance to the board office, which sat on the edge of the high school campus, he walked in the front entrance and greeted his receptionist before joining some of his administrative team in the staff lounge—a routine his staff had come to appreciate. After a few minutes chatting with colleagues, he made his way toward his office to start reading the vast number of emails that he knew awaited. Before sitting down at his desk, his phone rang. It was Ms. Brown, the high school principal.

Principal Brown

7:15 a.m.

Ms. Brown arrived at the high school and checked her emails to make sure substitutes were scheduled for the day. Returning to school after having a snow day would likely be more hectic than usual—checking missed assignments, adjusting lesson plans, and getting back into a routine—not to mention spirit day and preparing for homecoming festivities. "Whew, what a week!" she thought.

After she sent her daily staff memo, she began her morning rounds–walking the hallways as she checked on teachers, bathrooms, and students before the day officially began. Her assistant principals were scattered throughout the building supervising high-traffic areas, including the commons, cafeteria, and bus drop-off. The goal for her team was to complete rounds and meet back in the commons a couple of minutes before the bell rang.

Ms. Brown finished her rounds and started her walk to the commons. All of a sudden, she began to notice students running toward her. Not having heard the bell, she thought, "They must be running toward a fight in the parking lot." Her pace quickened as she maneuvered her way up the hallway toward the commons area, when she heard a student yell, "Shots!"

In her mind she thought, "Someone must have thrown a firecracker or something." Seeking clarification, she called an assistant principal who was outside on bus duty. To her shock he told her he thought there were actual shots fired. Instinctively, Ms. Brown's quick stride now turned to a sprint as she ran toward the commons.

Student Jessie

7:30 a.m.

Jessie, a junior at the high school, passed the long line of parents dropping off their children before he eased into his usual parking spot. Just like every morning, he parked his truck, grabbed his backpack, and headed into the school. Having forgotten it was spirit day, he glanced around the commons at all the themed outfits before finally spotting a couple of his buddies. Standing in the open space, like many students did waiting for the bell to go to class, he was thinking about how overly crowded the commons seemed.

Suddenly, he and his friends heard a loud noise. He thought someone must have popped some of the balloons that he had seen displayed that obviously went along with the themed events happening at school that week, but the sound continued.

Superintendent Smith

7:50 a.m.

As Mr. Smith picked up the phone, Principal Brown said, "I've got one down." Smith's mind began to race. His initial thought was this: "Okay, we have a teacher who has had a heart attack."

"There may be more," Ms. Brown said next. At that moment Mr. Smith's heart sank, as he knew she was not talking about a teacher but a shooter.

He responded, "I am on my way."

As he jumped in his car, Mr. Smith noticed the drive from his office to the high school was still packed with the traffic flow of students heading to school. He decided to take the service road instead. Realizing the gate was locked, preventing him from driving any further, he leaped from his car and ran toward the school building.

Approaching the gym, Mr. Smith frantically unlocked the door and proceeded to the upper gym lobby. His heart was racing as he noticed the typical hum of happy chatter had been replaced by an eerily quiet silence. The only audible sound was the buzz of the students' cell phones vibrating on the floor, which had apparently been dropped in their rush to flee the building.

Making his way toward the commons, Mr. Smith came upon the first victim as a teacher, instructional aide, and janitor were performing first aid. With dread, he looked to his left and saw another victim with Ms. Brown and two staff members who were administering CPR. Continuing to move forward, he saw a third victim across the commons with adults applying pressure to his injuries attempting to stop the bleeding. A fourth student was pulled into the guidance office, where counselors applied first aid to his wounds. It just so happened that one of the health service courses was taught by a nurse that day, so she was going from one victim to the next conducting triage.

Seeing that the victims were receiving aid, Mr. Smith yelled, "Where's the shooter?"

In response an adult yelled, "We don't know." Glancing around the commons Smith now saw a place where students had once gathered to talk and share stories, but it was now littered with books, coats, coffee, cell phones, and other debris. He honed in on a student's bag that contained a baseball bat; having no other defense, he grabbed the bat and began to run in the direction he thought the unidentified shooter may have taken.

Advancing down the main hallway, Mr. Smith slowed as he approached the first intersection and cautiously rounded the corner—no one. He continued forward and saw a student peer around the next intersection. He yelled, "Get into a classroom, lock the door, and do not leave!"

Continuing down the hall, Superintendent Smith moved toward a room with a door ajar and found two frightened students huddled in the back corner. He directed them toward an exterior door where a teacher was escorting students to a secure location.

Proceeding with his search, he entered another room and discovered a student clearly in shock, sitting alone at a desk staring forward. He again placed the student in the care of an adult, to be ushered to a safe location. Returning to the commons to check on the victims, he discovered the EMTs had not yet arrived.

Principal Brown

7:50 a.m.

As Ms. Brown raced to the commons, she saw a student down and realized it was an active shooter situation. Everything began to happen at once. She immediately called Superintendent Smith. As he answered, she said, "I have one down. There may be more." Quickly she began leading students to rooms, turning off lights, and ensuring doors were locked, as they had been trained to do previously that year.

Calling 911 became an impossible task. No calls could be made on cell phones because the network was instantly flooded with calls from students, parents, and teachers attempting to contact their loved ones. The landline proved no more effective as parents inundated the school with phone calls. There were no open lines. Each time Ms. Brown attempted to call 911, the line was taken by an incoming call, mostly parents desperate to know if their child was safe.

Recognizing communication by phone was impossible, Ms. Brown ran back to the commons and yelled, "I have to have help! I have cleared this area. I have to have help!" The technical school nurse happened to be in the building and heard her pleas. She summoned the assistance of the school nurse and other teachers who were not supervising students. Those individuals began to administer triage as they tended to the victims.

Students who were able to escape the school had rushed to safety, finding refuge in campus locations, buses, and even buildings across the street. Hardly anyone remained in the main building as Ms. Brown rushed to find the shooter.

The school resource officer, who had been supervising the parking lot for morning arrival, had seen students fleeing the school shouting, "Shooter!" He was able to reach authorities on his police radio and reported, "We do have a shooter; I need help."

Student Jessie

7:50 a.m.

As the popping sounds continued, kids started to duck and drop to the ground. After a brief hesitation, everyone began to run. Still rationalizing that the sound was just balloons for theme week and that everyone was running hysterically for no apparent reason, Jessie decided to "play along." Surely his classmates were "in on something."

Not knowing where his buddies had gone and whether there was any real danger, he began to run alongside another classmate. As they ran, stumbling over kids and bags lying on the floor, he lost his shoe. Not stopping, the two continued to run frantically, shouting to others, "What is going on?" Their hysteric minds could not understand what was happening.

Jessie and his classmate reached the exit door and stepped outside where he saw chaos unfolding—kids running to the highway, some jumping over the fences, and others knocking down small trees as they drove their vehicles through the yard. Jessie's truck was parked on the far side of the campus, and he figured there was no way he would be able to leave even if he could reach his car. So, they both headed toward the technical center, where they saw teachers ushering students.

Jessie, along with many other students, remained in the technical center for approximately an hour. He watched through the windows as a helicopter landed and a SWAT team entered the school. It was difficult for his mind to process what was happening around him.

Eventually, Jessie and the other students boarded school buses and were transported to the middle school, where his dad would be allowed to take him home. While waiting for his dad, Jessie began to call his friends to see if everyone was okay. It was at that time he discovered that his two buddies, whom he had been standing between in the commons, had both been shot.

Secure Site

Many students had dashed to the exterior buildings on campus to find a safe location amidst the chaos. School personnel escorted students to these presumed safe locations and remained with them to provide comfort and security. With everyone unaware, the shooter had filed in with the other students as they fled the high school.

While in lockdown, a couple of students approached one of the supervising teachers and said, "The shooter is in here with us." The teacher allowed the reporting students to leave the building to find authorities. Now, having the student in his sights, he could see that both his hands were in his pockets.

Not wanting to cause alarm and escalate the situation, the teacher discreetly made his way through the crowd to stand directly behind the identified shooter. As he made his approach, deputies who had been contacted by the students that had been allowed to leave the building, entered the facility. The deputies motioned for the student to come toward them, and without protest, the shooter willingly complied to their command.

Superintendent Smith

7:58 a.m.

What seemed like an eternity was, in reality, only minutes. The SRO, state and local police, and the county sheriff had arrived on the scene and were now in pursuit of finding the shooter and securing the premises. Word had reached Mr. Smith that two deputies had a suspect in handcuffs. He made his way quickly to the suspect. The deputies asked the student where the gun was located, and he told them where he had discarded it. The police were now able to officially secure the scene, and EMTs were allowed to enter the building.

Mr. Smith called his district staff and sent them to the middle school to help with the reunification of students and parents. He spoke with his transportation director to begin gathering as many bus drivers as possible—coaches, club sponsors, anyone certified to drive a bus to the middle school. Ambulances transported injured students—one student went to the local hospital and two students went to regional hospitals; two students were airlifted. Smith sent a member of his district team to each hospital, ensuring someone remained with the students until their parents arrived.

Later that day the governor arrived and held a press conference. Many organizations and religious groups offered their support. Smith addressed the faculty before they left for the day and had a time of prayer. It was determined that school would be dismissed the next day. The state's school safety advocate provided him with recommendations to consider following a tragedy. He found the information especially helpful in deciding when to return to school, how to clean the building, and how to support students, staff, and the community.

Principal Brown

7:58 a.m.

Ms. Brown surveyed the area where staff were caring for the victims. Since EMTs had not yet arrived, students and staff began to take those needing medical attention that could travel to area hospitals. Several off-duty first responders happened to be in the drop-off lane that morning and offered their assistance, in addition to the faculty and staff who were providing aid until EMTs were permitted to enter the school.

At this same time, Ms. Brown had received information that the shooter had been captured. She began to head in that direction, but when she saw that the sheriff deputies had the shooter and the gun, she felt it was best not to approach. Instead, she returned to assist first responders as they quickly began to work together. Now that the site was deemed safe, EMTs were beginning to tend to the health of those in need and airlifting those with more serious injuries.

Ms. Brown thought, "It is now time to switch modes," since hundreds of students were still in lockdown. Although the gates had been locked, parents parked on the street and began approaching the school, desperately wanting to enter the campus to reunite with their child. She, alongside some of the first responders, informed them that they were not allowed on the campus because it was an active crime scene. She explained to them the reunification plan and the procedure to pick up their child.

Ms. Brown met with all the teachers who were supervising students. She gave them papers and had them list the names of the students under their care, due to attendance not being recorded since the incident occurred before school began for the day. Teachers were charged with the responsibility to account for those students as they were transported to the reunification site. As this was occurring, police were diligently questioning student witnesses and taking statements. Even before she was able to reach the reunification location, Ms. Brown's cell phone had been bombarded by the media. News stations, not local to the area, had also gained access to her cell number.

At the reunification site, students were placed in the gym, where windows were covered to assist school staff in maintaining control in an orderly manner as parents and students were unified. The middle school served as an appropriate location since the locker rooms provided bathroom accessibility, and the stage allowed an isolated area for police to interview students.

Assistant principals had been sent to area hospitals to check on the status of the injured. Parents grew impatient at how much time was taken for them to have access to their child. Brown, with police escort, spoke to them, giving them assurance and explaining why it was a timely process.

Additionally, teachers were receiving emails and were unsure of how to reply. It was communicated to them that only PR personnel should respond. The staff needed guidance, as it was difficult to think clearly at that moment. The district office began sending one-calls. Once all students had been released to guardians, the staff was asked to write down their statements before returning home. Many did not have their purse, keys, or vehicle, since they were unable to reenter the school, which was now deemed a crime scene, so police helped transport everyone home.

Superintendent Smith and Principal Brown

10:30 p.m.

Mr. Smith and Ms. Brown went home briefly to change clothes, then headed to the hospitals where victims had been airlifted. They met with parents at the hospitals, where the state police had remained to prevent the media from approaching the families.

Returning home around 1:30 a.m., Brown began to read the books that had been delivered by the representative from the Center for School Safety in order to prepare a plan. At 4:00 a.m., she was finally able to rest before having to facilitate the staff meeting that would begin in a few short hours. It was shared with the staff that outside counselors were available for anyone that needed emotional support. Additionally, a staff person was assigned to each victim to ensure clear, timely, concise communication with each family.

Student Jessie

Jessie did not want to return to school. He preferred to go stay with a relative in another part of the state. His dad, though, did not feel it was a good decision to "run away." It was agreed that he would not attend school on Friday, but instead, he would wait until Monday to return.

Five Years Later

Jessie remembers that when students returned to school, the support dogs helped him to keep his mind off things. He acknowledged that he, and others, experienced a lot of grieving. For a while, he felt that he was just coasting. He said a lot of the events still seem to be a blur, but some things stand out in his memory. Students no longer gathered in the commons, metal detectors were installed, yet everyone was still on edge.

Jessie remembers other things, such as the candlelight ceremony and tons of community support that aided with the healing process. He remembers returning to school and seeing all of the parents and community members who held up signs conveying their love and support. He also noticed a change in the way teachers taught and cared for students post-tragedy and how they attended to the needs of students in a more intentional manner.

Regardless, Jessie says that day had a tremendous impact on him by instilling a fear that this type of incident could happen again, and not just at school. It is a resounding thought almost everywhere now, sometimes an uncontrollable fear. He often thinks, "What if . . . ?"

CHAPTER SUMMARY

A school is attacked by an early morning shooting, with several students injured and the perpetrator being a student as well. The courageous actions of students and school district leadership, including the principal, teachers, medical first responders, and law enforcement, de-escalated the emergency swiftly and saved lives.

QUESTIONS FOR REFLECTION

1. How do schools account for all students during a crisis when:
   a. school has not yet begun/roll has not been taken?
   b. during transition periods of the school day?
   c. reunifying after a crisis?
2. What is the plan when lines of communication are compromised?
3. What should be considered when communicating with multiple stakeholders regarding confidentiality and public records?
4. Think about your current staff. Who possesses the knowledge and expertise to administer aid to victims in an emergency situation?

Chapter 3

Panic at the Disco

Ann Burns

Leaders should think about themselves as islands of coherence in a sea of chaos. The ability to manage yourself in a crisis—it is important to stay grounded and clear in a situation that's totally disorienting.

—*Jeremy Hunter, PhD*

Dr. Brown glanced down at her watch, nervously anticipating the excitement of the next few hours. As a first-year high school principal, she had never experienced a school dance from the supervision perspective. Tonight would be another first during the new leadership role. As she walked around the old gym, she admired the job the homecoming decoration committee had done on transforming it into a "Night in Paris." She felt so lucky to have been selected to lead this school.

Mr. Carroll, the assistant principal, stepped in from the lobby. "Are we ready for the dance?"

Dr. Brown smiled and replied, "I think we are ready! Can you think of anything we are forgetting?"

"I think we have everything covered," he replied as he began one final look over the gym-turned dance floor. Dr. Brown had come to rely on Mr. Carroll's input, as he had been a teacher in the school before becoming the assistant principal—a role he had held for several years.

Additional faculty and staff began to arrive, preparing the lobby for student check in, marking students' names and capturing pictures as they entered the gym for the dance. Ms. Mitchell made her entrance dressed as a disco queen, accompanied by her husband who was dressed as Elvis Presley. One of the school traditions was for faculty to dress for the occasion at the dances, so in addition to formal wear, some faculty arrived in Scottish kilts, dressed as various movie stars, and one even in a "French toast" costume.

The collegiality of the small group made Dr. Brown smile. Parents were gathered outside to watch the students arrive and snap candid photos as they entered. "This type of parental enthusiasm could only be found in a small town," Dr. Brown thought to herself as she greeted parents, grandparents, and older siblings that had gathered for the annual event. Everything seemed to be going well.

A few minutes later, Kellie, a bubbly sophomore who lived down the street from Mr. Carroll, rushed up to the group and blurted out, "Mr. Carroll, I don't think Samantha Gadd is acting right. Can you come check on her?"

"Sure, Kellie. I can check on her, where is she?" Mr. Carroll replied.

"Samantha was going to the bathroom," Kellie answered.

Dr. Brown smiled and said, "Mr. Carroll, how about I go and check, since it is the bathroom? Kellie, lead the way."

As they rounded the corner to the bathroom, Dr. Brown saw Samantha lying on the floor. She rushed to the student's side and began checking for vital signs. The pale, fragile looking girl was breathing; however, she was not responsive to her name. A small crowd had begun to gather around the group. Dr. Brown sent Kellie directly back to get Mr. Carroll.

The time seemed to be in slow motion as Samantha continued to lay motionless on the floor. When Dr. Brown asked about her date or friends that may have accompanied her, it seemed no one knew. The faces looking back at Dr. Brown had the same expression of fear reflected in her own face.

As if on cue, Dr. Land, who was still in the building dropping his daughter off at the dance, appeared beside the motionless teenager. He looked directly at Dr. Brown and said, "I am a doctor, may I evaluate her?"

Recognizing him from previous school events, Dr. Brown was happy to see him, as a feeling of relief washed over the new school administrator's face. "Yes, would you please?"

As Dr. Land knelt over the student, Samantha had become a little more responsive and proceeded to throw up all over her formal gown and Dr. Land as he tried to turn her head to keep her from choking. After examining the situation, Dr. Land indicated he felt it would be in the best interest of the student if she were taken to the hospital. Dr. Brown immediately agreed, using her cell phone to dial 911.

Once that call was made, Dr. Brown proceeded to use her phone to look up the emergency contact information for Samantha. This was a call she dreaded making but knew it had to be done.

As the telephone was ringing, Dr. Brown prayed that Samantha would be all right and wondered how this could have happened. Remaining calm and polite, she informed the mother of the medical emergency. Mrs. Gadd was overwhelmed with emotion. She was at a soccer game with her son, and her husband was working out of town. She assured Mrs. Gadd she would be there as soon as possible.

The ambulance arrived, and the EMTs evaluated Samantha. They strapped her to the gurney and wheeled her to the ambulance. Dr. Brown discussed the situation with Mr. Carroll and the other faculty sponsors. They would continue to chaperone the dance while Dr. Brown followed the ambulance to the hospital to ensure that Samantha was okay.

Dr. Brown followed the ambulance to the emergency entrance and watched as the gurney was unloaded. By the time the EMTs got the gurney on the ground, Mrs. Gadd rushed up and grabbed Samantha's hand. Dr. Brown was happy to see that she was responsive to her mother. That was a good sign. With the arrival of her mom, Dr. Brown felt that Samantha would be taken care of, and she needed to begin the process of finding out how this happened.

As she left the parking lot, she met Mr. Whitaker, a judge in town. His children were also high school students at the school. Hopefully, nothing was going on with them.

Returning to the dance to try to begin the process of investigating how Samantha arrived at the school in the condition she was in, it quickly became clear to Dr. Brown that the students were not going to talk about who arrived with whom and where they had been before the dance. They were only interested in continuing the dance fun now that Samantha was going to be okay.

The next morning, Mr. and Mrs. Gadd arrived at school to discuss Samantha and any repercussions from her actions at the dance. They informed Dr. Brown that Samantha was diagnosed with alcohol poisoning, and the hospital had pumped her stomach, started an IV, and watched her for the evening before allowing her to be released.

Surprisingly, Mr. and Mrs. Gadd did not understand why there should be consequences for Samantha. After all, she was the one who had to go to the hospital. Dr. Brown referred the parents to the school handbook and policies related to after-hours school functions and they then agreed with a three-day suspension. The parents did share the names of the other students with whom Samantha attended the dance. As it turned out, she was the date of Judge Whitaker's oldest son. Samantha and his daughter were in the same class, and Samantha was dating the older brother. Dr. Brown realized this prom couple was where to start questioning.

By the end of the day, it was clear students nor parents were interested in uncovering how a fifteen-year-old student could have alcohol poisoning. The timeline for Samantha prior to the dance included meeting another couple and going to Judge Whitaker's house for pictures. The students involved and the judge remained silent regarding the past evening's events. One lone student informed Dr. Brown of an afternoon of heavy drinking at one of the homes of the students, but there was no one to corroborate this information.

With increasing frustration, it became apparent that the only consequences would be to Samantha, who seemed to have suffered enough. Next steps included a faculty meeting to discuss the incident and review procedures for dances to ensure a safe and secure environment for all students.

CHAPTER SUMMARY

A new school administrator experiences a student medical emergency at a school dance. The ensuing investigation reveals that political power and privilege outside of school sometimes affects the consequences of inappropriate behaviors. The principal weighs the limited options for discipline when parents and students do not assist with investigating underage drinking off school property.

QUESTIONS FOR REFLECTION

1. What processes are in place to ensure after-school events are in compliance with school safety policies and procedures in your building?
2. What would be the best-case outcome for this case study? Why?
3. What policies could be developed to ensure after-school events are safe and secure for all students?
4. What is the political impact of the involvement of the judge? If you were the superintendent of the school district or building principal, how might you respond?

For more information related to underage drinking, please visit the following websites:

- Substance Abuse and Mental Health Services Administration: https://www.samhsa.gov/talk-they-hear-you/parent-resources/what-you-can-do-prevent-your-child-drinking
- National Institute of Alcohol Abuse and Alcoholism: https://www.niaaa.nih.gov/publications/brochures-and-fact-sheets/underage-drinking
- Interagency Coordinating Committee on the Prevention of Underage Drinking: https://www.stopalcoholabuse.gov/

Chapter 4

Phrases

Keith Griesser

"Be mindful when it comes to your words. A string of some that don't mean much to you may stick with someone else for a lifetime."

—Rachel Wolchin

The most powerful way to keep a school safe does not come in the form of a metal detector, an eye-catching poster on the wall, a cute acronym, or even a well-written school safety policy. No, the most powerful way to keep a school safe is by creating a culture where everyone in and associated with the building takes responsibility for maintaining the safety of the people. The gold standard of school safety takes a collaborative effort from students, teachers, and other stakeholders. In this chapter we will look through the eyes of Max to explore three common phrases that have a direct impact on a school's culture of safety: "Don't be a tattletale," "Snitches get stitches," and "See something, say something."

As school administrators, we should create systems where students, staff, and other stakeholders are comfortable proactively addressing safety concerns. We should create an environment where there is a collective mindset that we are all responsible for the safety of one another. However, too often, we use a common phrase to relay a vastly different message to our youngest and most vulnerable students.

PHRASE #1: DON'T BE A TATTLETALE

"Don't be a tattletale!" Seth yelled to his friend as Max began running toward the first-grade teachers gathered under the shade tree on the side of the playground. Seth knew he had cut in line, but he did not want to get in trouble. Max was mad, but he did not push Seth out of line because he did not want to get in trouble either. Instead, Max went to the nearest adult he could find.

However, as he approached the teachers, one of them called out, "Max, you're not here to tattle, are you?"

Max stopped running and simply replied, "No." He put his head down and slowly turned around to go back to the line. He was confused, disappointed, dejected, and downright mad. He thought he was doing the right thing by going to an adult. He thought his teacher would hug him and thank him for using his words instead of getting into a fight. But there was no such reception. As Max reached the back of the line, Seth, who was still at the spot in the front where he had cut, pointed at him and laughed.

The next day as the class lined up to go to the cafeteria for lunch, Seth cut in front of Max again. Without hesitation, Max shoved Seth out of the line. Seth fell and hit his head on a desk. The teacher came running over to make sure he was okay. Max was sent to the principal's office. The principal called his dad to come to school. Max was so mad, he was shaking and could barely speak. He was finally able to angrily say, "Dad! Seth cut in . . . " But his dad cut him off and said, "Son, you need to take responsibility for your actions and quit being a tattletale."

After the meeting, the principal had Max's dad take him home for the rest of the day.

The biggest danger with the phrase, "Don't be a tattletale," is that it is used by so many people that kids trust! Parents commonly use it when they do not want to hear the endless whining and bickering from their children. Teachers use it, especially those in younger grades like the one in the story above who were dismissive of Max. Kids like Seth, who know they have done something wrong but do not want to get in trouble, use it. In fact, this phrase is voiced so often that children begin to believe that it is true; convinced that they are on their own to try to resolve these types of issues.

Despite adults saying they want to help, their actions tell a different story. The result is that we are destroying our most valuable school safety asset when we use the phrase, "Don't be a tattletale." Even more concerning, it is not just schoolyard bullies who use this phrase. Child abusers, predators, and other individuals with bad intentions will say, "Don't be a tattletale" to the children they abuse. We are, in fact, perpetuating a victim mentality in our youngest, most vulnerable students by dismissing them in times when they need adult assistance in dealing with a situation by misusing a simple little phrase, "Don't be a tattletale."

Questions for School Leaders: Don't Be a Tattletale

1. How can we ensure that students in our care are receiving support in working through situations they are not yet equipped to handle on their own?
2. How can we support teachers who do not have time to address every student report individually?

PHRASE #2: SNITCHES GET STITCHES

Years later, Max was in a freshman physical education class. He was changing in the locker room when he heard a commotion coming from the shower area and went to investigate. When he got there, Max saw Seth standing by the toilet, giving a swirly to a much smaller kid. A couple of Seth's friends were standing by laughing at the scene. After Seth let the student up, he and his friends approached Max. One said, "What are you looking at, punk?" The other said, "You best be on your way before you get dunked, too." And then Seth said, "And don't even think about telling, Max, because snitches get stitches."

Max had stopped going to adults in his school long ago, and he knew that it was not worth the risk to tell this time either. Max decided to wear gym shorts under his jeans so that he would not have to go in the locker room to change ever again. Though he was sure that Seth would continue to bully other students, Max felt helpless to do anything about it. He had internalized the phrases, "Don't be a tattletale" and "Snitches get stitches."

Questions for School Leaders: Snitches Get Stitches

1. What are the areas in your school where students do not feel safe because there is lack of supervision?
2. Does your school have an anonymous tip line for reporting school safety concerns? Do students know how to get to the tip line?

PHRASE #3: SEE SOMETHING, SAY SOMETHING

Fast forward two years. With COVID-19 forcing everyone to learn from home during their sophomore year, adjusting to being back in person for school had not been easy. Kids and adults were more stressed, and anxiety levels were higher than before the pandemic. People talked about mental health and how even superstars like Olympic gymnast Simone Biles were struggling. But other than a daily announcement over the intercom mentioning self-care and a new emergency help line (988 in Kentucky), everyone was still expected to push through and figure it out on their own.

Max knew something was up with Seth. While Seth had always been mischievous, something seemed different this year. They'd had several run-ins in the past, starting back in elementary school, but Max had never seen Seth this agitated and angry. Today, Seth was super amped up. Max thought he had either consumed too many energy drinks or maybe even taken drugs before school.

Then Max overheard Seth say that he had a gun in his truck. Max could not hear the rest of the conversation, but he was already panicking. With all the school shootings lately, he wanted to tell someone what he had heard, but he had many internal questions: Is there a way to report this anonymously? What if Seth were just showing off and didn't really have a gun? Would people think Max was just trying to get back at Seth for incidents in their past? If he really had a gun and found out that Max was the one who told, would Max become a target? What if Max had to testify in court? But sadly, it also occurred to Max that he didn't even know an adult he trusted enough to notify.

After taking a deep breath, it came to him. Max knew who he could tell. He trusted his fifth period teacher, Mrs. Mahone. She was the faculty leader for his advisory/mentoring class. They had weekly talks about everything from school assignments to his scores on the archery team. She even helped connect him with a grief counselor after his grandpa passed away. She had always said that her job as his advisor/mentor was to try to help him with anything life threw at him, whether that be academics or anything else. He knew she was the person he could trust.

Max found Mrs. Mahone and they moved to a private space where Max shared what he had heard.

Immediately, the school was placed on lock down, as the police officers found a hunting rifle and a hit list with twenty-five names written on it in Seth's truck. The news that night reported that a firearm was found on the school campus and praised an anonymous tip for most likely saving many lives that day.

Mrs. Mahone never told anyone where she received the information. She understood the level of trust it took for Max to confide in her. She also understood the importance of the confidentiality by which she was bound as an education professional. But most of all, she understood that the key factor in school safety is developing relationships where students can overcome thoughts like, "Don't be a tattletale" and "Snitches get stitches," and instead, embrace the wisdom of "See something, say something" to a trusted adult.

CHAPTER SUMMARY

A student is repeatedly discouraged from reporting behavior that breaks school rules, and one day comes face to face with a possible planned school shooting. Fortunately, he has been in an advising/mentoring class, and that teacher provides the support he needs to come forward in time.

QUESTIONS FOR REFLECTION

1. What processes are in place within your school that allow students to report safety concerns?
2. Are your students aware of the process of reporting a safety concern? When was the last time you asked a student specifically what they would do if they saw or became aware of a safety issue?
3. When will you speak with your staff about the importance of confidentiality when it comes to student reporting of safety concerns?
4. What other common phrases come to your mind that might send the wrong message to students and educators regarding creating a culture of school safety? (For example, "Not my circus, not my monkeys.")

Chapter 5

Community Disaster

Abbigail Morris

> *A person's leadership is often best gauged when a crisis is in progress. At crunch time, those with maturity and wisdom will step in and provide support and solutions.*

Nine days after Susan had accepted the position as interim principal, a record-breaking tornado hit her school community on a Friday evening. The heart of the city was leveled. The path of the tornado ripped through the city, county neighborhoods, and industrial parks. The destruction was massive. The hours, days, and weeks after the tornado were focused on finding loved ones, securing housing, restoring electricity and municipal services that were destroyed, and ensuring community services, such as religious services, would be available.

Individuals from all over the country were pouring into the rural community to assist with debris removal, donation logistics, and distribution. Teams of educators who were able to help were clearing debris from roads, houses, and businesses; organizing distribution centers; and supporting disaster relief efforts. The school buildings were turned into shelters, warming places, distribution centers, Christmas stores, and churches. The district turned into a receiving center for donations and tried its best to help manage the flux of items that were pouring into the city. In addition, the district was trying to contact all the families it served.

Administrators in the district worked to identify which families in their schools were hit by the tornado, where they were living, and what needs they had. Every school and every department within the district had members that were impacted—loss of home, damage to home, trauma from being in the path of the tornado, or worse—loss of a family member.

Sarah, walking through her school gym, was struck by the large amount of donated clothes that had been tediously unpacked. Every box and bag of donated clothes were sorted so families could come in and easily grab what they needed. She walked through her commons area, just two weeks ago filled with holiday decoration, now a floor to ceiling food pantry.

Multiple truckloads of donations were being unloaded into the school. Beyond the building being used for donations, it hosted government agencies who were helping individuals apply for unemployment, lost identification documents, and other services provided to communities directly following a natural disaster. The culinary and cafeteria kitchens were being used to prepare food for volunteers in the community.

Susan worked with the outgoing principal as they kept the building open at night to allow the volunteer electricians, linemen, and heavy equipment operators the opportunity to shower in the basketball locker rooms. The district had called off classes for the remaining week of the first semester.

After Christmas break, Susan was relieved to know school would start second semester as scheduled. She called her leadership team (assistant principals, guidance counselors, and resource officers) together for a meeting prior to students and staff returning. She wanted to hear concerns, as well as ideas, on how to welcome everyone back. Additionally, she wanted to set the tone for what they could expect from her as the interim principal.

Susan started the meeting by thanking everyone for their time and efforts over the past several weeks. She stated her goal was to support the transition of school leadership and needed the leadership team to support her in maintaining the same expectations and routines that the students and staff had come to expect with the previous principal. Sarah wanted to bring the staff together for block meetings on the first day back to introduce herself, reassure the staff of her expectation, and hear from and support them as they worked with students. She reiterated to her leadership team: "We have to assume everyone in our school community is experiencing trauma."

Susan then turned the meeting over to her leadership team to allow them to share ideas on how to support the school community, ensure routines were re-established, and to reinforce expectations. Mr. Grey, the guidance counselor with the most years of experience, shared stories that he had heard from students who volunteered in the rescue and recovery efforts. He suggested that the school share signs of trauma with the teachers so they could feel more confident to report students who might need additional support. Ms. Perry, another guidance counselor, suggested creating a survey for every student to complete during the first period on the first day back to help the team identify those who needed immediate support.

Mr. Rose, an assistant principal, wanted to make sure that the school prepared families and students for the monthly safety drills, which he felt would be a potential trigger for some students and staff. The team agreed that providing clear communication to families and faculty about upcoming drills ahead of time and providing families with guidance on how to support their children during this recovery time would be appropriate.

Ms. Simpson, another assistant principal, addressed the faculty concerns about grades. Since the school was unable to finish the last week of the fall semester, students were unable to complete their midterms and finals. The team determined that those scores would be forgiven, and any necessary tests would be given after a couple of weeks of review and reorientation with the assessed curriculum.

At the block meetings, the leadership team discussed trauma and the counseling plan. Several teachers had questions. Ms. Black raised her hand. "What do I do if students want to talk about what they went through? I just don't feel comfortable, especially if they say something inappropriate or misguided."

Mr. Grey readdressed the staff. "We do not expect, nor desire you to counsel students in the classroom. It is okay to let kids talk about the tornado if you are comfortable with that; however, one of the best things we can do for our students is to establish routines to which they are accustomed in our classrooms and pay attention to students who you believe are behaving out of the ordinary. When you suspect something might be wrong, please complete the counseling form, and we will set up a time to talk with the student. If you feel they need to see someone right away, please call the counseling office. Understand that trauma may impact students differently, and you can help us by being the eyes and ears of the school."

Mr. Bowling raised his hand, "What about students who are just trying to get out of class and say they have to go to counseling?"

Susan responded by sharing the process through which students would go who had appointments for counseling. "Teachers and guidance counselors will have to work together to support students. While we will do our best to minimize the impact of the students being out of the classroom, we all can recognize the importance of this time with the counselor."

FURTHER CONSIDERATIONS

In the above scenario, Susan is dealing with two major disruptions to her school community. The first and most pressing is the devastation that happened to her community. The second is a change in leadership during the middle of a school year. She has to be aware of both factors as her leadership team considers their moves to re-establish the culture of the school.

As Susan and her team move forward, it is important that they understand the impact trauma can have on students, teachers, and the school community.

Trauma can be defined as a response to an external event or series of events whose outcomes have negative consequences beyond what a child's normal coping skills can deal with (McInerney & McKlindon, 2022).

Due to the unpredictable nature of a tornado and its destruction, kids can feel a sense of guilt or unjustness which might develop into unrealistic thoughts about why or why not the tornado hit their home. The faculty and staff at Susan's school need to understand that a child's recovery will be influenced by the adults in their life and how those adults handle the stress of the situation. Discussion of the events should be done with factual and honest information; time should be allowed for students to process what has happened; and most importantly, routines should be kept as regular as possible (The National Child Traumatic Stress Network, n.d.).

Ms. Perry's suggestion to gather information as soon as possible through a survey is an excellent way for the school to understand more about each student's experience and to begin to respond to the needs of specific students. Trauma impacts individuals differently. Some students will exhibit certain behavior changes, while others may appear to have no behavioral problems. Children who are exposed to stress too often or too long, such as those who live in chronic poverty or adverse living conditions; are neglected or abused; and/or separated from parent(s), can have poor responses to dealing with stress (National Scientific Council on the Developing Child, 2014).

The first step in recovery is to identify those students who are unable to cope with the trauma. Trauma can lead to delayed brain development and learning issues. Research has shown that the brain develops well into young adulthood, and as a result, trauma during these formative years can be particularly harmful. Beyond the neurological changes, trauma can lead to learning and behavior issues (The National Child Traumatic Stress Network, n.d.).

When Susan addresses her staff on the first day of the new semester, her guidance team shares some possible signs that teachers could look for in students who might be having a hard time dealing with the traumatic event. Children struggling with traumatic response can appear to display some of the following: discomfort with feelings, depression or anxiety, behavior change, trouble with self-regulation, difficulties relating to others, regression of prior skills, attention deficits, academic challenges, nightmares, difficulty sleeping and abnormal eating, physical aches and pains, dependence on drugs or alcohol, and other increases in risky behavior.

It is estimated that one in four children will experience at least one traumatic event in their lifetime. Encouraging teachers to anticipate potential challenges following a traumatic event allows the school community to provide additional support to the children in need in a proactive manner. Outlining how children will receive counseling and processes for providing children safe places to talk is important, as it allows students to share in a nondisruptive "safe space" and provides the educator with clarity around actions to take.

Research conducted by Bryan Rivera showed that teachers are not always aware of what counselors are trained to do, and their perceptions are not always accurate. Teacher involvement and collaboration is fundamental to successful counseling implementation (Rivera, 2011).

In the above scenario, Susan has the counselors present at the period meetings to help educators understand the skills, training, techniques, and services that counselors can provide and the benefits those services have on learning outcomes. Having the counselor serve as part of the leadership team supports the importance of the work counselors do for the school community.

Immediately after a natural disaster, schools play an important role in supporting the community through recovery and a path to well-being. Reopening schools after a disaster helps to re-establish normalcy and routines for families (Lai et al., 2019).

In addition, schools can provide learning opportunities for students and the community on disaster preparedness. Organizations such as the Red Cross offer opportunities for teachers and youth to create clubs that support community preparedness.

Schools can be used for shelters, distribution centers, and/or command posts for various organizational entities dealing with the aftermath of the disaster during natural disasters. During natural disasters, principals and other school leaders can be called on to provide leadership in a variety of ways to the larger community. Being prepared, and understanding the role of the school within the community management plan, will help provide confidence during such events.

CHAPTER SUMMARY

A new interim principal is faced with a catastrophe when her school and community suffer major damage from a severe Friday evening tornado. The devastation makes headlines across the country. The quick action taken, and recommendations for future consideration, lend key insight.

QUESTIONS FOR REFLECTION

1. In the scenario above, how might you address the staff as they return to school after a natural disaster? What would be your talking points, and why do you feel those would be essential to share with your staff?

2. How would you involve parents in the support of your students as they navigate the potential trauma associated with a natural disaster?
3. As a new principal, how might you support your school with trauma-informed classrooms?
4. Establishing a trauma-informed team is essential to support the school when events like a natural disaster occur. Who would you include on your team and why? How would you share the work of the trauma-informed team with the school community?
5. Dealing with traumatized students requires collaboration between teachers and counselors. How might you increase the interaction between these stakeholders? How would you clarify the counselor's role for teachers?

REFERENCES

Lai, Esnard, A.-M., Wyczalkowski, C., Savage, R., & Shah, H. (2019). Trajectories of school recovery after a natural disaster: Risk and protective factors: School recovery after a natural disaster. *Risk, Hazards & Crisis in Public Policy, 10*(1), 32–51. https://doi.org/10.1002/rhc3.12158

McInerney, M., & McKlindon, A. (n.d.). Unlocking the door to learning: Trauma-informed classrooms & transformation schools. *Education Law Center.* https://www.elc-pa.org/resource/unlocking-the-door-to-learning-trauma-informed- classrooms-and-transformational-schools/

Meier, K. J., O'Toole Jr., L. J., & Hicklin, A. (2009). I've seen fire and I've seen rain: Public management and performance after a natural disaster. *Administration and Society, 41*(8): 923–53. https://doi.org/10.1177/0095399709349027

National Scientific Council on the Developing Child. (2005/2004). *Excessive stress disrupts the architecture of the developing brain: Working paper 3. Updated Edition.* http://www.developingchild.harvard.edu

Rivera, B. (2011). *Teacher perceptions of the American School Counselor Association's national model in an urban setting [published master's theses]. SUNY Brockport.*

The National Child Traumatic Stress Network. (n.d.). *Tornado Resources.* Retrieved January 10, 2023, from https://www.nctsn.org/what-is-child-trauma/trauma-types/disasters/tornado-resources

Chapter 6

Not in My School

Chuck Hamilton

It's better to hold those we lead accountable than assuming they will police themselves. Even highly trained professionals are notorious for getting themselves into harmful and unethical situations.

Well, there are much better ways to end a holiday break from school. Superintendent Willis had been enjoying a little less stress over the past few days, actually spending time with family and enjoying some time in personal reflection—something a school superintendent rarely gets to do when schools are in session. A few days before classes were to start after break, she received a phone call with information no school administrator wants to hear. The caller wanted to remain anonymous, which always made Dr. Willis a little nervous and also skeptical. And after the call concluded, she knew she would need to immediately initiate some communications and begin an investigation.

The caller began with the dreaded statement, "You have a teacher carrying on an affair with one of your high school students!" Dr. Willis listened as the caller laid out what he claimed to have witnessed on multiple occasions at school events and at different times in the community. She carefully took notes as the caller, somewhat animatedly, shared his thoughts on what he had witnessed. While documenting, separating each reported event as an individual act, she could not help but wonder what initially made the informant start putting these isolated events together to draw such a serious conclusion. After twenty minutes of listening, with interruptions limited to affirming what was said by the caller, Dr. Willis asked the question, "What made you believe these events were connected and more than what they seem when viewed separately?"

The caller told her his child played ball with the student involved and had expressed at the start of the season "something funny" was going on between the student and faculty member. Since many of the reported incidents were at the school's athletic facilities and parking lot, it made sense that a parent might be alert to the sum of the observations. Dr. Willis assured there would be an investigation and asked for patience and confidence in the process.

After hanging up, she took a few minutes to reread her notes and consider what next steps should be taken. On the one hand she wanted to immediately protect the student, even if he did not understand he was being manipulated—if this was indeed actually happening. The uncertainty of the accusations also meant protecting the faculty member from the potential of a false report or misunderstanding that had the ability to ruin her career and personal life.

THIS CAN HAPPEN ANYWHERE

According to the Kentucky Department of Education (KDE)'s Kentucky Educator Credentialing System (KECS) data compiled by the KDE Office of Legal and Legislative Services, over the period 2009 through 2021, there was an average of 1,706 reports per year to the Standards Board involving educator misconduct, and of those an average of 2.15 percent was around sexual misconduct.

Too often, communities believe these improper relationships only happen in other places, when in reality, they can and do occur in just about every school setting. What makes it hard to fathom is that it is often good teachers who are well thought of in the school and by the community. Every incident of an inappropriate student-teacher relationship is not by predators or psychotic teachers. Perpetrators are often caring, committed teachers who are experiencing a difficult time in their life and who is in contact with a needy student. The teacher does not set appropriate boundaries for the relationship and consequent results are detrimental to the student, teacher, families, and community (Fibkins, 2006).

WHAT ARE WE GOING TO DO?

After some thought and reviewing board policy and state regulations on reports of this nature, Dr. Willis contacted the faculty member's immediate supervisor and asked to meet with him the next morning—a day that turned out to be a marathon of investigations. She and Principal Thomas met in her office, and she explained, "I have had a concern brought to my attention from a community member about a possible inappropriate relationship between a student and faculty member."

Mr. Thomas was shocked and said, "This is not possible in our school district. I just don't believe this."

"Just listen to the report in its entirety, and then we can discuss rationally." After hearing the concerns, without naming the faculty member or student, Mr. Thomas knew which student and teacher were being reported. He hung his head, and Dr. Willis could tell he was struggling with the accusations and possibilities they raised.

After a few moments of silence, Mr. Thomas wearily asked, "What are next steps?" This led Dr. Willis to believe her principal was now second guessing his own observations and wondering how he had missed something right in front of him.

Mr. Thomas opened up. "The teacher in question asked for the student to be assigned to her classroom as a student-worker for one period a day at the start of the school year, which we do as part of our internship program." He followed up with how he now recalled times the student was in the teacher's classroom after school, particularly on days the team had late practice or an away game.

Shaking his head, Mr. Thomas said with remorse, "I even recall commenting to the teacher how impressed I was with their dedication to the team, school spirit and all." He added that these did not seem like problems before the accusations, but now he was second guessing himself.

"Take a deep breath. Remember we will work with facts, not assumptions, so do not jump to a conclusion before we have exhausted our investigation." Dr. Willis decided the report was going to require additional research but should be limited to those who might have personal knowledge of any concerns. She divided the work, with the principal contacting the coach and a trusted faculty member who taught on the same floor.

Dr. Willis contacted the board chair to inform him of the investigation, as was policy and practice on events that could lead to legal action or community backlash. She made the decision to not discuss the accusation with the parents or talk to the student until there was more information, a triangulation of data so to speak. This was compounded by the need to take action to protect the student as soon as possible, as school would be back in session in two days.

Dr. Willis decided to review game tapes from the season to date and to look at video recordings from the high school parking lots, which was how the rest of the day was spent. She made every effort to keep the investigation as low key as possible, knowing if it turned out to be false, the damage to a teacher's reputation could be irreversible. While viewing tapes, she received a call from the teacher who Principal Thomas had contacted, who wanted to talk to her personally about what she had shared with the principal. It was a difficult conversation, as the teacher was now mortified that what she had been seeing was starting to make more sense, and she was worried she had not reported concerns earlier.

"No one wants to be involved with something like this, especially when you can find ways to justify what you see or hear as just an involved teacher," Dr. Willis said with compassion. Basically, the trusted teacher shared hearing what she now saw as inappropriate "teasing" and "joking." She also shared seeing the student "help" the accused faculty member by holding her around the waist as she stood in a chair to hang papers in the classroom. The teacher also shared how the classroom door was frequently closed after school, and she could hear the boy and accused talking in low voices.

Similar to Superintendent Willis's own suspicions when the caller was reporting all these seemingly isolated situations, the trusted teacher just did not put them all together until asked. Now she was mortified she had possibly perpetuated something illicit by not saying anything. The trusted teacher indicated the student never seemed to be in distress or upset. In fact, he seemed to really enjoy "helping" the teacher in question and "hanging out" in the classroom. Dr. Willis thanked the teacher for her cooperation and cautioned her to be patient and trust the process. She reminded her that the district policy stated that no school employees as witnesses were to discuss matters under investigation with anyone other than their immediate supervisor, or law enforcement if required.

As the day was drawing to a close, Dr. Willis had seen enough game film to assure the teacher in question and student had a close relationship, even to the point the teacher often sat with, or very near, the family of the student at ballgames. This by itself was not a problem but did support the belief they had a more involved relationship than what might be typical of teachers and students.

The parking lot video was not sharp in many cases, but again, there was evidence the teacher had been in the student's car briefly several times after games, and on at least one occasion they had left for a period of time—returning to their car when the parking lot was empty. Again, the evidence did not specifically show anything illicit but did reveal some obvious problematic behaviors that would need to be addressed.

Superintendent Willis and Principal Thomas got back together to compare notes and decide on next steps. Dr. Willis made the decision to talk to the suspected teacher first thing Monday morning when the faculty and students returned. Sunday, she tried to put things out of her mind and focus on family, but something this serious just could not be ignored, and her mind kept turning with the possibilities. Was this more a lack of professionalism that could be addressed through a reprimand and additional training? Is this not only a breach of professional ethics but potentially illegal, requiring the involvement of law enforcement? How will we assure the community of the safety of students if this turns out to be worst case? Will we be able to protect the integrity and trust of the faculty member if it is simply poor professional decisions?

WHAT SHOULD YOU KNOW

Curating the development of professional leaders in the United States requires a commitment to ethical and moral standards. In fact, the Professional Standards for Educational Leaders (PSEL) explores ten standards of leadership expectations. Among them, standard 2 states, "Effective educational leaders act ethically and according to professional norms to promote each student's academic success and well-being" (NPBEA, 2015).

PSEL standard 2 is further defined through indicator (f), which states the leader will "provide moral direction for the school and promote ethical and professional behavior among faculty and staff" (NPBEA, 2015), thus clearly indicating the expectation for school leaders to address the potential for even the most heinous of actions proactively. This is additionally illustrated by the Model Code of Educator Ethics in Principle III-A(8), which states, "The professional educator respects the rights and dignity of students by: Acknowledging that there are no circumstances that allow for educators to engage in romantic or sexual relationships with students" (NASDEC, 2015). How can the expectations for educators be stated more clearly in relation to inappropriate student-teacher relationships?

So, where do we start to protect our students from these psychologically and often socially harmful experiences? Fibkins (2006) says, "There is simply a lack of training, supervision and intervention—which leaves administrators, teachers, and students at risk." The subject cannot be ignored, and current practices do not adequately address the needs. We cannot rely on everyone doing the right thing in these situations when there is obviously a disconnect. Newspapers and other media sources are full of stories and reports, many like you are reading here.

HOW WAS YOUR MORNING?

Monday morning rolled around, and Superintendent Willis made her usual drop by the office just as busses were leaving to begin morning pick-ups. She wanted things to appear as normal as possible until she knew exactly what she was dealing with this day. She and Principal Thomas had already decided the teacher in question would not be reporting to her classroom and had a substitute come to the school without knowing the assignment until arrival.

Every effort to protect the employee and student in the event the accusations and suspicions were not as severe as they had the potential to become was being taken.

Dr. Willis was in the school conference room a little before the time most teachers began arriving, and Mr. Thomas was waiting near the teacher's classroom to intercept her and walk her to the conference room. Dr. Willis greeted the teacher with a smile and asked her to have a seat. "Would you like a bottle of water?"

Dr. Willis then also sat down and quietly said, "I am going to ask you something, and I need you to know I would not ask if I did not already know the answer." The teacher nodded and looked at her expectantly as she was asked by her CEO, "Is there something you need to tell me, so I can help you work through the problem?" The teacher took a big breath and over the next thirty minutes confessed everything. She said, "I even recall you talking to us about this [teacher-student relationships] on our opening faculty day and me looking around the room thinking, 'Who would do that?' and yet, here I sit."

Without going into details, as they are not necessary at this point, the situation was worst case. The relationship started innocently enough, but as the teacher and student shared more about one another's personal lives, it just evolved and was hard to stop. The student involved was not a minor, which eliminated a call to law enforcement. However, the breech of educator ethics was such that a report was made to the state certification board, who conducted their own investigation and took appropriate action.

The teacher was asked if there was anyone she wanted to call after the meeting, as there were concerns for her emotional well-being at this point. Principal Thomas sat with her until a family member came to pick her up. Superintendent Willis contacted the parents of the student involved and asked to meet with them that morning if possible, and they agreed to meet. As she drove to their home, she thought of how she would react to this type of information if she was the parent. She wanted them to know their child was top priority, and the district was taking immediate action to address the issue with all involved.

CHAPTER SUMMARY

A school superintendent is faced with accusations toward one of her teachers that point to an inappropriate relationship with a student. She first talks to the teacher's principal and takes the necessary actions to make sure everyone involved is protected, but also held accountable.

QUESTIONS FOR REFLECTION

1. How do you balance the rights and privacy of the accused with the safety and anonymity of the student in these cases?
2. What could be done to eliminate these types of incidents in your school/district?
3. What will communication look like to the faculty, board members, press, community, parents, accused, and the student?

REFERENCES

National Association of State Directors of Teacher Education and Certification. (2015). Model Code of Ethics for Educators (1st Ed.). Retrieved January 4, 2023 http://www.nasdtec.net/?page=MCEE_Doc#PrinI

National Policy Board for Educational Administration. (2015). Professional Standards for Educational Leaders 2015. Author.

Chapter 7

We Have a Runner

Neely Traylor

For any educator, there is nothing more stressful than when a student goes missing. Hundreds of "routine" days and "routine" decisions suddenly disappear in an instant when a child has fled the "camp."

Nearing the end of the school day, administrators heard through their radio, "We need an administrator to Mrs. Jones' room." Dr. Taylor, school principal, made her way to the classroom where she was met at the door by a visibly distraught Mrs. Jones.

"Logan left my classroom, and he is not in Mrs. Hughes' room." Mrs. Hughes was the special education teacher with whom Logan worked throughout the day. Dr. Taylor immediately got on the radio to see if anyone had seen Logan in the hallway. No one responded that they had, and all administrators, counselors, and custodians immediately began checking all bathrooms in the building. With no luck, the assistant principal, Mrs. Graves, used the intercom to call a soft lockdown. Teachers knew that this meant they needed to keep all students in the rooms but that there was no danger in the building.

Administrators also did an "all call" for the student to come to the office. Logan did not return, and administrators did not have any luck locating him. At this time, administrators, counselors, and special education teachers began checking outside areas—the playground and all around the building, but to no avail. It was determined that the school had a runner, and that Logan was not on school grounds. Unfortunately, it was dismissal time, and the buses were lined up in front of the school.

Dr. Taylor quickly assigned staff to continue with the dismissal process and immediately had the front office call Logan's guardians to let them know that he had left school grounds. Another office staffer was assigned to call the school resource officer and local police to alert them that a student had left the school grounds. The scariest part was that no one was sure how long Logan had been out of the building and in what direction he had gone.

Administrators and special education teachers began spreading out away from the campus, looking in yards and down streets. Calls began to come in from residents in the community that they were seeing a young man that matched Logan's description in an area close to the school. Some school staff were on foot going door-to-door, and others were in vehicles going up and down streets. They were calling Logan's name, trying to get a response to locate him. Later it was determined that this was ineffective, as he was running further away when he heard voices.

This frantic door-to-door, street-to-street search went on for what seemed like an eternity. Information was coming from a number of sources confirming sightings of Logan in different areas within blocks of the school. The resource officer and a number of local police were circulating the streets near the school, and Logan's guardian had joined the search. The school was getting calls that Logan was in the creek in between two streets and that his shoes and coat were found there. It was so hard for the search party to not think the worst.

After what seemed like an eternity, but was actually twenty-eight minutes, Logan was located in a nearby field where the school resource officer and local police officers were able to surround him in their patrol cars. The feeling of relief was visible, and the guardian was immediately contacted to let them know of Logan's location.

After a tearful reunion and lots of "thank yous," Logan was released to his guardian. Before leaving the scene, Dr. Taylor spoke with her, sharing her concerns about Logan's behavior and the need to take the next day to set up a detailed plan for his safety. Dr. Taylor explained this would be a principal-excused absence and would allow the adults responsible for Logan's safety to meet. She also discussed resources the family might consider in order to address their social, emotional, and behavioral concerns. Logan's guardian shared that Logan had run away the past weekend and that she now wished she had shared this information with the school. Thankfully, she was very understanding and was not upset with school personnel in any way.

Meanwhile, students and parents at dismissal were left in very competent hands but were wondering what was going on and if it involved their own kids or siblings. As soon as Dr. Traylor returned to the building, she sent a social media message sharing only what information was needed—a student had left campus and had been located. She thanked the community for sharing their sightings of the student and apologized for any inconvenience caused.

Parents and guardians were very thankful for this information, and only one parent was upset that he did not get the information quicker. Dr. Taylor was able to explain that the priority at the time was to locate the specific student and to notify the guardian immediately.

After letting everyone breathe and decompress from the incident, later that evening, Dr. Taylor texted the adults involved in the incident—administrators, counselors, classroom teacher, and special education teachers—to praise their quick efforts and obvious concern for Logan's welfare and to request a meeting the next day to debrief and develop a plan specific for him.

The next morning, a very relieved team of educators met to discuss the events that led up to this very scary situation and to determine what could be done better if something similar occurred again. The school already had a detailed safety plan; however, after this traumatic event, it was obvious that other measures needed to be put in place for this specific type of emergency and for this specific student.

So, what did the group discuss and learn from the incident? In this meeting, it was shared that a bus driver actually saw Logan come out an exterior door and texted a school counselor. The school counselor did not see this text until after Logan was found because the staff was communicating via radio. It was decided that any time this type of event occurred in the future to call the front office to share such urgent information. The team also discussed that Logan was able to run for a lengthy amount of time because school personnel were yelling for him, and he could hear them.

The group determined that anyone searching should not be shouting the student's name in a future instance. The need to begin searching outside the building immediately, rather than everyone looking within the building, was also discussed. Finally, the team devised a plan for this student in which he would be escorted at all times by an adult in the building for all transitions throughout the day. They also requested a meeting with the guardian for the next day to discuss the new plan prior to Logan returning to school.

CHAPTER SUMMARY

A student disappears, and the principal and staff kick into emergency mode and find the child quickly. Afterward, the debriefing on what went well and what could be improved upon in the protocol for "next time" offers invaluable "lessons learned" for any school.

QUESTIONS FOR REFLECTION

1. Do you have a specific procedure within your safety plan to address actions that would be taken if a student leaves your campus? Does this plan identify detailed action and who is responsible for these actions?
2. Who is aware of this plan? Do you include bus drivers, cafeteria staff, and other classified personnel?
3. Do you have a clear communication plan that identifies how information about such an event will be shared with parents/guardians/community?
4. Do you have a clear procedure/expectation for debriefing such an event, and does it include a meeting with parents/guardians to discuss the safety plan for their student?

Chapter 8

The Apple Did Not Fall Far from the Tree

William Ingle

> *The influence a parent has on a child cannot be measured and will surface more and more as the child grows and develops tendencies for how to deal with the decisions and stressors of life.*

It was a Monday morning in October. The school day at Pine Needles Middle School started decently. Other than the office staff having to find a substitute for one of the mathematics teachers on short notice, the school day had been rather quiet. Every chance he gets, Principal Ansel Brody likes to walk the halls, visit classrooms, and be a visible presence among the students and staff. The first lunch period was about to start. As he often did, Principal Brody made his way toward the cafeteria. As he approached the cafeteria entrance, the volume of the students' talking changed noticeably.

Before he even reached the cafeteria entrance, Principal Brody could tell that a student altercation had erupted. He made a beeline for the two boys tangled up on the floor and flailing at one another. Mr. Martin, a social studies teacher and assistant coach of the middle school football team, reached the two fighting students before Principal Brody did. Mr. Martin pulled off the larger of the two boys, who was atop the other and throwing wild punches at his opponent on the cafeteria floor.

Principal Brody helped up the other boy, who had sustained a bloody nose. Having separated them, the two men took the perpetrators to the office. Mr. Martin took one to the school nurse for his bloodied nose. Principal Brody took the other boy to his office to start sorting out what happened.

Principal Brody was already familiar with one of the students. Scotty Penrond—the student who bloodied the other student's nose—had been referred to his office twice this academic year for reports of his bullying other students. Per the school district's policy, Principal Brody issued a warning and conferenced with Scotty and the school counselor after the first incident, which occurred in August.

The second incident, occurred in September, led to a disciplinary referral, lunch detention, and a phone call to his parents. Now, Scotty had gone from bullying to fighting, and Principal Brody wanted to understand why the two boys were fighting. Scotty responded to Principal Brody's questions rather cagily, saying he did not know why the fight occurred, but that the other student, Ricky Smith, had started it.

Mr. Martin, whose duty assignment was in the cafeteria that day, reported that he saw Ricky go to the table where Scotty was eating lunch. Mr. Martin observed Ricky and Scotty talking but had no idea what the increasingly heated conversation was about. As Mr. Martin started to make his way over to the two boys, Ricky started to walk away. Scotty started to rise and grab Ricky's arm. Ricky pulled his arm away from Scotty, pushed him back into his seat, and again started to walk away. Scotty jumped up from his chair and attacked Ricky. Although lasting only seconds, Ricky had sustained a bloodied nose in the scuffle.

Having received care for his bloodied nose, Ricky Smith was questioned about the incident. Like Scotty, Ricky also responded rather cagily at first, simply stating that Scotty was the one who started it. One of the students seated at the table had subsequently come by the office to report that the boys were talking about a knife just before the fight broke out. When pressed why Scotty attacked him, Ricky said that he learned that Scotty had a butterfly knife and was going to report it to the office. As Ricky tried to leave, Scotty grabbed his arm in an effort to prevent him from going to the office. With this information, Principal Brody became quite concerned about the potential presence of a weapon.

The school resource officer (SRO), who was at another campus that morning, drove to the middle school. The SRO searched Scotty's coat and patted him down in the principal's office, but the officer found nothing. He then searched Scotty's locker and did indeed recover a butterfly knife. When pressed with this information, Scotty confessed to having the knife, but that it was Ricky's, and he was just holding it for him.

At first, Ricky vehemently denied this, saying it was Scotty's knife and not his own. Scotty eventually confessed to getting the knife from Ricky, who was going to sell it to him for ten dollars. Scotty took the knife from Ricky right before the start of first period but refused to pay him the ten dollars. Ricky protested. Scotty responded by telling Ricky that he would pay him later in the day. Ricky had come to the cafeteria to press Scotty for his money. When Scotty refused to give him the ten dollars, Ricky threatened to report the knife to the office. Scotty sought to prevent this, and a fight escalated from their interactions.

Having explained the details of what transpired between the two students, both boys were subject to the school district's policy and behavior matrix for fighting and weapons possession, which called for out-of-school suspensions, parent meetings with the school administrator, and the weapon being turned over to the local sheriff's office. Principal Brody called both of the boys' parents. Ricky's father was upset but acknowledged that his son had knowingly taken it from their house and, thus, would have to be responsible for his actions. The principal and the SRO released Ricky to his father.

Scotty cried and begged Principal Brody not to call his father because the call would wake him up and he would be angry. Scotty said his dad worked the night shift at the local oil refinery and would be sleeping. Principal Brody responded that he had no choice but to do so. Mr. Penrond was indeed asleep when the principal called him. The father responded angrily, asking, "What has Scotty done this time?" After Principal Brody gave a brief synopsis of the situation to him over the phone, he indicated that he was on his way to the school.

Mr. Penrond arrived at the middle school and the school receptionist buzzed him in. She led him back to the principal's office where Scotty, Principal Brody, and the SRO were waiting for him. Scotty continued to cry, looking at his father fearfully. Mr. Penrond strode up to his son angrily and violently struck him across the face. Although shocked, the SRO responded quickly, grabbing the father and separating him from his son, who was visibly shaken by the blow. His face started to swell at the point of impact. Principal Brody thought to himself, "No wonder Scotty is prone to violence. Apparently, the *apple did not fall far from the tree.*"

CHAPTER SUMMARY

A principal deals with a fight between two boys and models how to get other appropriate staff involved and contacts the parents. He is reminded that students typically inherit their misbehavior patterns from their parents.

QUESTIONS FOR REFLECTION

1. In cases involving student searches, courts seek to strike an appropriate balance between the public school district's legitimate interest in

maintaining a safe and appropriate learning environment and a student's reasonable expectation of privacy protected by the Fourth Amendment (Brady et al., 2021; Colwell et al., 2017). Given the scenario above, do any of the actions taken by the principal or the SRO raise concerns?
2. In the scenario described above, both of the male students involved in the fight received out-of-school suspensions. Neither of the students were identified as qualifying for special education services within the district, but if one (or both) were receiving special education services, how might this have affected the consequences they received?
3. School employees have a duty to protect children in their care and to report child abuse—whether as an eyewitness, having direct knowledge of child abuse, or becoming aware of the possibility of child abuse through rumor, innuendo, or second-hand reporting (Gessford, et al., 2017). How should the principal and SRO respond to what they witnessed?

REFERENCES AND SUGGESTED READINGS

Brady, K. P., Ingle, W. K., & Pijanowski, J. (2021). Searches in public schools: Contemporary legal considerations for educators. In L. Stedrak, & J. Mezzina (Eds.), *Legal literacy for public school teachers*. Education Law Association.

Colwell, W. B., Brady, K. P., & Ingle, W. K. (2017). Searches in public schools. In J. Decker, M.

Lewis, E. Shaver, A. Blankenship, & M. Paige (Eds.), *The principal's legal handbook* (6th ed.). Education Law Association.

Gessford J. B., Perry, G. H., & Knight, J. J. (2017). Child abuse. In J. Decker, M. Lewis, E.

Shaver, A. Blankenship, & M. Paige (Eds.), *The principal's legal handbook* (6th ed.). Education Law Association.

Chapter 9

Kentucky Office of the State School Security Marshal

School Safety and Resiliency Act of 2019

Ben Wilcox

> *Schools are not malls. Adhering to increased safety policies is a critical piece in decreasing school violence and intrusions.*

The School Safety and Resiliency Act of 2019 was signed into law on March 11, 2019 (Kentucky Revised Statue 158.441). The bill was written as a comprehensive approach to creating the safest Kentucky schools as possible, not only utilizing security measures but also focusing on student mental health. The focus on mental health places a strong emphasis on student relationships with school employees as trusted adults, one in which students feel comfortable not only reporting issues they are facing at school but also sharing situations they are encountering in their personal lives.

The Office of the State School Security Marshal was created through the passage of the School Safety and Resiliency Act. The Marshal's main function is to enhance school safety by monitoring safety initiatives, developing reasonable training, and performing onsite, unannounced risk assessments at all public, locally controlled schools within the Commonwealth of Kentucky.

Regional compliance officers are tasked with completing the onsite review of the risk assessments and supporting the school's compliance with the mandates set forth by the bill. They also serve as a resource for the school by making recommendations on how to structure a safe and secure learning environment. The compliance officers also make referrals to the Kentucky

Center for School Safety for training and consultation on specific issues faced by the school.

SCENARIO

A father comes to visit his child several times a week to eat lunch and volunteer in the classroom. He has never shown any indication of hostility or malice during his visits to the school and is seen by staff as a loving and vested parent in his child's well-being. Due to his frequent visits, the office staff often allow him to enter the school without first speaking with him. One day he arrives two hours before the child's lunch hour. The office staff see him in the parking lot and electronically unlock the building's front door before he reaches the intercom.

The door opens, and the father becomes visibly upset. He charges past the front office and heads toward his child's room without signing in with the office staff as required. He has made it to the child's room, and since this incident takes place prior to KRS 158.162(3)(d)(5), the classroom doors are open and unlocked during instructional time. He walks right into the classroom. While this is happening, a law enforcement officer arrives at the school and advises school officials that the parents of the child have had a domestic altercation requiring emergency response.

This type of scenario would cause a disturbance inside the building and could lead to potential harm of students or staff.

What mandates set forth by the School Safety and Resiliency Act assist in mitigating the danger to students and staff?
 a. KRS 158.162(3)(d) requires controlled access to the building while school is operational and in session:
- The main entrance of the school must be locked and unlocked electronically and be equipped with cameras and an intercom system.
- All visitors are required to report to the front office, provide valid identification, and state the purpose of their visit.
- All visitors must be provided with a badge that must be visibly displayed on an outer garment at all times while inside the school.
- Classroom doors are required to remain closed and locked during instructional time.
- Outside access through exterior doors must be controlled during the school day.

By adhering to the above mandates, the control/locking of all exterior doors and locking of classroom doors during the school day provides a layer of protection from exterior and interior threats. Utilizing electronically locking doors, intercoms, and cameras allows gatekeepers to identify if a visitor should be allowed entry inside the building while also assessing their demeanor prior to entry. If a visitor makes it past the office check-in process but is later determined a threat, the closed and locked classroom doors will keep children and staff safe.

The School Safety and Resiliency Act also provides student access to mental health services and mental health professionals, including the law requiring a school resource officer to be assigned to all Kentucky public school campuses. These mandates were established to assist students and staff in obtaining assistance and treatment before a traumatic event arises. The bill requires threat assessment teams, which is a proactive approach to address student issues before harm is done to other students or themselves.

A ratio of one mental health professional to every 250 students is recommended as funds and personnel become available. Trauma tool kits have been distributed to schools. The Handle with Care program is available to all schools, public or private, throughout the Commonwealth. Active shooter response training is required for all student-contact staff [KRS 156.095(7)], and suicide awareness training is required for all student-contact staff and provided to all students [KRS 156.095(6)]. Additionally, parents, staff and students have access to a statewide anonymous reporting tool to report threats to law enforcement.

School resource officers (SRO) are required to have 120 hours of training prior to being certified as an SRO and serving in a law enforcement role. This professional development not only encompasses active shooter and firearms training but also trains an officer on how best to work with students and staff in a school setting—including students with special needs, trauma-informed care, and diversity awareness [KRS 158.4414(7)]. This training makes SROs one of the most specialized units in law enforcement.

CHAPTER SUMMARY

The mandates set forth by the School Safety and Resiliency Act have been enacted to ensure schools and students are safe from internal and external threats. The Office of the State School Security Marshal verifies and assures mandates are followed and assists all Kentucky public schools in need of help so every child can focus on learning, growing, and developing in a safe and nurturing environment. Our youth are our leaders of tomorrow and deserve to learn in safe school settings.

QUESTIONS FOR REFLECTION

1. Since the passage of the School Safety and Resiliency Act, have safety protocols restricted access to your school?
2. Is safety and security more prevalent at your school and enforced by front office staff, knowing that an assessment will be conducted yearly by the Office of the State School Security Marshal?
3. Has there been an increase in safety-related discussions and trainings provided to staff for professional development?
4. Do students and staff feel safer since the passing of the School Safety and Resiliency Act? If so, in what ways?

REFERENCE

Kentucky Revised Statue 158.441. (2019). SB 1 School Safety and Resiliency Act. Kentucky Department of Education. (n.d.). Retrieved from https://education.ky.gov/school/sdfs/Pages/School-Safety-and-Resiliency-Act-%28Senate-Bill%2019%29.aspx#:~:text=In%202019%2C%20the%20Kentucky%20General%20Assembly%20passed%20the,many%20agencies%20that%20work%20with%20districts%20and%20schools

Chapter 10

Fear of the Unknown

Brett Burton

When it's crunch time in a crisis situation, the leader is often faced with more than one option and only seconds to make critical decisions. There is no time for gathering the team for a vote.

Dr. Clarke was in his fourth year as a middle school principal and his eighteenth year as a school administrator. He had previous experience as an elementary principal, high school assistant principal, and athletic director. As an experienced school leader, he was trained in crisis management, including active shooter response training. Even though he encountered many unique school crises during his career, this particular day will always be remembered.

On Friday, February 15, 2019, at 2:05 p.m., Dr. Clarke decided to step away from his desk while writing a teacher summative evaluation, as the March 1 deadline would arrive soon. He informed his secretary, Ms. Johnson, that he would take a walk in the school hallways and return after the middle school students' four-minute transition period, which began at 2:06 p.m.

The veteran principal made visibility between passing periods a priority. The building was calm despite the excitement of a three-day weekend. Although Dr. Clarke's leadership team was reduced from four to two, his dean of students, Mr. Soto, managed to supervise three lunch periods with no student discipline. Today was a good day—only two class periods remained, as 3:38 p.m. was right around the corner.

On this particular Friday afternoon, administrative presence during transition periods was essential. Since Dr. Clarke's two assistant principals were absent, he and Mr. Soto were the only two administrators in the building. In addition, Dr. Clarke was tired, as the day before had been Valentine's Day, and the middle school students had enjoyed an after-school dance until

6:00 p.m., with the last student not picked up from school until 6:45 p.m. However, he was in good spirits on this Friday afternoon, as student dismissal was less than two hours away. The only after-school event was a sixth-grade girls' basketball game.

As Dr. Clarke walked the hallways of his middle school, he greeted students and teachers, assisted a few sixth graders with opening hallway lockers, and raised his voice to inform students not to run in the hallway, which was a daily occurrence. Finally, the 2:10 p.m., eighth-period bell rang, and the kids were in their classrooms. Immediately after the transition, a radio call came from one of the assistant superintendents from the central office, stating, "Attention all building principals. Please copy." Dr. Clarke stepped into an empty office at the south end of the building to receive information from the district office.

The word "copy" was code for principals to respond that they heard the message and were tentatively listening for the next message. The district, located in the western suburbs of Chicago, had seventeem schools (ten elementary, four middle, one high school, one preschool, and one alternative educational center). All seventeen school leaders responded at various times.

Next, the school district's assistant superintendent, Ms. Karen White, commanded that all schools be placed on "lockdown." Ms. White followed the "lockdown" directive with this statement: "Principals, it is vital that students and staff remain in their current classrooms, following lockdown building procedures. Also, outside agencies, or visitors in your schools are prohibited from leaving. Please make sure no visitors are allowed into the building, including parents and volunteers. We have a dangerous threat in the community and will send more information once it is available from law enforcement."

All seventeen school leaders stated their names and school and responded, uttering the word, "copy." During the radio transaction, one of the elementary principals asked what she should do about dismissal (elementary dismissal time was 2:20 p.m.), as parents and school buses were already waiting outside her school. White stated that parents and buses must wait until the district office provides an "all clear" command. Dr. Clarke became more concerned, with the threat level so high that elementary schools could not dismiss students and teachers.

After receiving the directive, Dr. Clarke switched radio frequencies, transitioned to channel one, and requested Mr. Soto meet him in the main office. As an experienced school principal, Dr. Clarke was adept at utilizing distributive leadership. Bolman and Deal (2017) claim that effective "leadership is distributed rather than concentrated at the top" (p. 336). He realized he would need additional support from Mr. Soto and his teachers. The current emergency was extremely vague and did not include pertinent information to explain why the building was in lockdown. Fear of the unknown covered the school community.

Next, Mr. Soto, who had heard the directive from Ms. White on his radio, quickly walked to the main office. Dr. Clarke looked at Mr. Soto, "I have no idea." Mr. Soto responded, "This is so bizarre."

Then, Dr. Clarke read the prepared lockdown script over the intercom: "Please excuse the interruption; we are going into an all-school lockdown. No individuals should be in the hallway, restrooms, or common areas. Anyone in the hallway or transitioning should immediately go to the nearest classroom until further notice. Teachers, if you have any emergencies, please use the intercom and request an administrator to come to your classroom. Again, we are in lockdown until further notice. Thank you for being so cooperative."

Dr. Clarke started the distribution of leadership action steps. He directed Mr. Soto to begin sweeping the hallways and checking classroom doors. Mr. Soto asked if he had received any information from the school resource officer, Mr. Stone. Dr. Clarke shook his head "no" but informed Mr. Soto he would text him once he provided Ms. Bean and Mrs. Curtis, the two office staff, with directions about visitors and parents attempting to pick up their children for any appointments.

Mr. Soto started sweeping the building. Dr. Clarke asked to see the main office visitor sign-in and sign-out sheet to determine who was in the building. Then, he went on the radio and requested that Mr. Flores, the eighth-grade algebra teacher and athletic director, who was finished teaching for the day, to come to the main office.

Since Mr. Flores was a member of the building crisis team, and the building's two assistant principals who were also members of the crisis team were absent, he could support Mr. Soto with sweeping the hallways and checking classroom doors to make certain students and staff were complying with lockdown procedures. Next, Dr. Clarke sent a text to Officer Stone to see what was happening in the community. Officer Stone did not respond, which was uncharacteristic and caused concern.

Mr. Soto, Mr. Flores, and Dr. Clarke circulated the hallways and checked the classroom and exterior and interior doors. All three school personnel communicated over the school radio that the hallways were clear and classroom doors were secure. At that time, the three met at the interior rally point, located outside the gymnasium doors away from the classrooms. The time was 2:30 p.m., and the building was eerily quiet. Mr. Soto asked Dr. Clarke, "Any word from Officer Stone?" Dr. Clarke responded, "No."

During the conversation, they heard many loud, blaring police sirens. As the sirens were blaring outside, Ms. Karen White from the district office came on the district radio frequency and stated, "Attention, building principals, do you copy?" At various times, all seventeen principals stated their names and responded, "Copy."

At approximately 2:40 p.m., Ms. White stated that an imminent threat was taking place in the area and to please remain in lockdown until further notice. Still, schools at this time were not being directly threatened. The seventeen school principals responded by stating their names and "Copy." Dr. Clarke looked at Mr. Soto and Mr. Flores and said, "I still have no clue."

Mr. Soto stated, "I am going back to my office to see if local media has posted any information. I will let you know if I hear anything."

Dr. Clarke agreed, and added, "We will continue to sweep the building and check on students and staff."

The eighth-period bell was going to ring in a few minutes. As Mr. Flores walked the school hallways, one of the teachers opened her door and asked if students could use their Chromebooks during this time, as they were getting bored and impatient. This was the first year all students in the school district had one-to-one technology. Mr. Flores radioed and asked if students could use their Chromebooks. Dr. Clarke felt this request may help teachers maintain safe and orderly classrooms. Thus, he agreed, but he later regretted this decision.

The eighth-period bell rang, and all students and teachers calmly remained in their classrooms. An eighth-grade teacher, Ms. Twitty, contacted Ms. Johnson in the main office and requested Dr. Clarke come to her classroom. He stepped away from his desk, walked down the hallway, and knocked on her door.

Ms. Twitty opened the classroom door with her laptop in hand and said, "Dr. Clarke, there has been a mass shooting two miles away at the Henry Pratt Company (Moritz-Rabson & Phifer, 2019). Information has been posted on the 'patch' website about the factory shooting and possible deaths of workers. The students are aware of the incident. Should we restrict students from using technology? We may have parents or family members of students that work at Pratt."

Dr. Clarke was taken aback. He had not considered this aspect of the crisis. Once he gathered his thoughts, he told his teacher that he would draft and send an email to all staff to monitor student technology use. In addition, he stated that the email would include information about the mass shooting. Ms. Twitty shook her head in agreement and said, "Okay." The worried principal stood outside the classroom for a moment before returning to his office, second-guessing his decision.

Dr. Clarke drafted an email to all staff explaining that he was informed that a mass shooting had occurred at Henry Pratt Company, approximately two miles from campus. Still, he did not have any additional information. In addition, he informed the faculty that he would keep them posted on any new information. Also, his email stated that if students or staff needed to use the restroom, they should press the classroom "call" button, allowing teachers to communicate with the main office. Ms. Johnson would radio Mr. Soto and Mr. Flores to escort students or cover the classroom for teachers to use the restroom.

At 3:20 p.m., eighteen minutes before the dismissal bell would ring, Ms. White called on the radio stating, "Attention all building principals. Please copy." All seventeen school principals responded "Copy" over the radio one at a time. Then, Ms. White shared that the lockdown was over, and the threat had ceased. The local police had issued an all-clear. The community threat was over.

Subsequently, Ms. White asked principals to check their email immediately for information on the challenges with student transportation. Elementary students and teachers were one hour past normal dismissal; the high school was twenty minutes past dismissal. Thus, transportation would need to pick up at the elementary and high schools first. Ms. White estimated that buses would arrive at the four middle schools at the earliest, between 5:00 p.m. and 6:00 p.m. Dr. Clarke thought to himself about viable options. However, the most important priority was communicating to teachers and students that the lockdown was over.

He walked to the office intercom and made the announcement; however, he requested that all students and staff remain in their classrooms until the dismissal bell. After the announcement, he radioed for Mr. Soto and Mr. Flores to return to the main office to discuss options for the supervision of students who utilized district transportation.

Dr. Clarke had to think about what he would do with the approximately 450 students in his building that were transported to and from school by district transportation. Teachers were under no obligation to remain after school with students, as their contractual day ended at 3:45 p.m.

When Mr. Flores and Mr. Soto arrived at the main office, Mr. Soto shared that Ms. Bivens, Mrs. Gord, and Mrs. Klein were highly upset with his decision to allow technology to be used during the lockdown. All three teachers wanted an explanation. If they did not receive an answer, they would contact the district office, specifically the superintendent. They believed Dr. Clarke's decision to allow student use of technology was insensitive and poor leadership.

Dr. Clarke understood and informed Mr. Flores and Mr. Soto that he would email the staff members that weekend to schedule a meeting first thing on Tuesday morning to explain his position. He hoped the teachers' anger would subside after the three-day weekend. Mr. Soto suggested Dr. Clarke take a few minutes and briefly explain to the teachers the rationale for his decision.

Dr. Clarke declined the counsel, as his priority was ensuring all students safely arrived home. Teacher dismissal was at 3:45 p.m., which meant that he and Mr. Soto would have to supervise 500-plus students until 5:00 or 5:30 p.m. Dr. Clarke radioed Mr. Franks, the building custodian, and asked him to make sure all the bleachers in the gymnasium were rolled down and prepared for students.

Dr. Clarke began calling bus riders by grade level to the gymnasium: "Attention, teachers. Thank you for your cooperation and outstanding work during the lockdown. First, students that walk home or are picked up by parents, please remain in your classrooms until the dismissal bell. Also, sixth-, seventh-, and eighth-grade students who are bus riders, please go to your locker, grab your personal belongings, and report to the gym. Please check in with Mr. Soto when you arrive at the gymnasium."

After the announcement, Dr. Clarke walked to the gym, and a few minutes later, the dismissal bell rang. The middle school students walked to the gym and were seated in the bleachers by grade levels. The time was 3:45 p.m., and the students were in the gym using their Chromebooks and conversing. Dr. Clarke and Mr. Soto informed the students that transportation would arrive sometime around 5:00 p.m. Students were to remain in the bleachers until further notice. A few students came down from the bleachers and asked Mr. Soto if they could use the restroom, call their parents, or walk home.

As Mr. Soto addressed their requests, Dr. Clarke noticed the three disgruntled teachers with their bags in hand walking toward him with negative body language and upset faces. Ms. Bivens, the veteran of the group, in front of students and Mr. Soto, said aloud: "You handled this situation wrong, Dr. Clarke! I had students in tears when they learned about the mass shooting two miles away! They were terrified and anxious! We are contacting the district office and setting up a meeting for Tuesday morning. Shame on you!"

Dr. Clarke stood in the gym and looked at Mr. Soto in shock. Mr. Soto shook his head and offered support, "Don't worry about it. Emotions are high right now."

After what they all had been through that afternoon, the veteran principal was dumbfounded. "I will contact Ms. White [the assistant superintendent] and give her a heads up. Also, I will email all three teachers this weekend and set up a meeting with them and their union representative. This is unreal."

Dr. Clarke and Mr. Soto remained in the gym with students waiting for their bus. Transportation started arriving about ten minutes after 5:00 p.m. The last bus arrived at 5:45 p.m. Once all the students were picked up and safely on their way home, Dr. Clarke went to his office and emailed the three teachers to request a meeting for the following Tuesday at 8:00 a.m. He encouraged them to bring union representation.

CHAPTER SUMMARY

During a school community crisis, a seasoned middle school principal finds himself without two assistant principals. The information about the crisis is vague, without any details provided to explain the district office directive to go into lockdown and wait until further notice. The principal attempts to assist his teachers by permitting students to use technology devices to maintain an orderly environment. Three teachers are visibly upset, because a mass shooting has occurred two miles from campus. Students learn about the shooting through social media and become visibly upset. The teachers threaten to go to the district office and inform the superintendent about the poor decision making of the principal.

QUESTIONS FOR REFLECTION

1. Does your school have any procedures or protocol to pause Internet/Wi-Fi use during a crisis?
2. Do you think Dr. Clarke handled the situation appropriately? Should Dr. Clarke meet with the teachers on Tuesday to address their disagreement in how the lockdown was handled by the administration?
3. How should Dr. Clarke address the three teachers on Tuesday? Should he be concerned with how the teachers confronted him in the gymnasium in front of students and Mr. Soto? Does Dr. Clarke owe the teachers and faculty an explanation regarding student use of Chromebooks during the lockdown?

REFERENCES

Bolman, L., & Deal, T. (2017). *Reframing Organizations* (6th ed.). Josey-Bass.

Moritz-Rabson, D., & Phifer, D. (February 15, 2019). Who is Gary Martin? Aurora shooting suspect identified by police. *Newsweek*. Retrieved April 2023 https://web.archive.org/web/20190217062007/https:/www.newsweek.com/who-aurora-mass-shooter-1333550

Chapter 11

Enraged Student

Veda Stewart

School safety is paramount for leaders to prioritize, as every student must feel safe in their environment to have optimum opportunity to learn. Mental health challenges for students become safety challenges that school leaders must be empowered to address in order to deliver on their promise of providing a safe space and place for teachers to teach and students to learn.

A frantic alarm radiated from the walking talkie. "Ms. Goodwin and Mr. Brown: Code 3, Code 3 to Ms. Johnson's classroom." This was the internal school message for 911. The administrators were in a leadership meeting and immediately dropped what they were doing and made a hasty trek to Ms. Johnson's classroom.

As they entered the K–3 hallway, the principal, Mrs. Barnes, witnessed a line of second graders walking toward her. The look in their eyes said everything. It was one of fear and anxiety that children should not have to experience. Mrs. Barnes ached inside, as she was supposed to be the one who protected them.

As she and her assistant principal got closer to the classroom where the disturbance was taking place, a student in the hallway, Holly, was crying and holding the side of her head. The paraprofessional attending to her, Ms. Monica, explained she had been hit by an object thrown by her classmate.

Apparently, Holly was the victim of an enraged child who had become violent in the classroom. Her face was red, and there appeared to be a growing bump and marks on the side of her head. Ms. Monica comforted her as she rushed the victim to the clinic to be checked out.

When Mrs. Barnes and her assistant turned the corner at the end of the hallway, the door of the classroom was ajar. They could hear yelling and screaming of obscenities coming from inside the room. As she and her assistant entered the door, more defiant language was spewed. "I don't care, I don't care! Leave me alone. Shut up—! You are stupid."

The teacher, Ms. Johnson, was trying to talk to the child, but in his heightened state, the student was oblivious to what she was saying. At first observation, the teacher seemed to be trying to de-escalate the situation, but in fact was enraging the student further. She was elevating the outburst by yelling back at him. It was clear that both teacher and student were not in control of their emotions and the tension was escalating rapidly.

The boy, Harrison, continued to berate Ms. Johnson while ripping the beautifully curated bulletin boards off the wall. Desks were turned over and chairs littered the room as he continued his rant in an out-of-control state. Mr. Brown, the behavior coach, had arrived a few seconds after the administrators, and they all looked at each other as they surveyed the situation. It was determined through gestures that they would form a safe bubble around the child.

At this point they decided to remove Ms. Johnson from the room. The circular bubble protected Harrison from harming himself and others. Mr. Brown began to show the boy how to breathe slowly in and out with techniques that he and the student had been practicing.

As the student began to calm himself, he kept repeating through his whimpers, "I didn't do anything." Once Mr. Brown could see that Harrison was in a better composed state, he sat with him and eased him out of the rage. The adults compassionately listened to Harrison's soft cries and waited for the calming down stage of his episode. This was not the first incident with Harrison, as there was a behavior intervention plan in place with the student.

This type of scenario plays out in multiple classrooms around the country. Yet this episode was a severe one because an innocent bystander had been physically hurt in the classroom encounter. The story of Harrison is not an isolated case of an enraged child in the midst of a heightened state where an innocent student is injured.

Harrison, like so many others who are unable to self-regulate, had emotional issues and trauma that were undiagnosed and became a real threat to school safety. This type of unchecked mental health can become an instant danger to everyone in the pathway of the emotionally damaged student— including themselves. Mental health plays a huge role in our school safety conversation, because when students do not have the ability to maintain self-control, it can turn into violent acts against others.

Harrison's mother was called, although, she had refused to support the school in the past. She was not happy to be called while at her job. She told the principal that the school needed to take care of the discipline at school, and she would deal with her son when he got home. She refused to come to the school until after work for fear of being fired.

The parent of the child that was hurt came to the clinic and wanted immediate answers.

She was livid and demanded to know what was going to be done to protect her child. She was not going to bring her child back to the school to be hurt again. She knew the other child in the class, as they lived in the same community. She said enough was enough and something had to be done. She wanted to press charges against Harrison. The staff assured her the situation would be handled, but because of confidentiality they could not discuss other students. This parent left the school very upset and called the central office to have her child removed from the school.

Harrison began to talk about self-harm after the incident in the classroom. The school social worker performed a threat assessment. It was recommended that the child receive in-patient care. His mother later arrived at the school but refused in-patient care for her son. She eventually agreed to outpatient care for Harrison. Sadly, this scenario would not end here but would become a lengthy battle of mental health challenges for the young boy.

Administrators have to spend a great deal of their time dealing with behavior and safety plans. In this case, room clears were practiced with students, and escape plans to exit quickly were in place. Many team discussions, parent calls and data collecting, calls to the classroom and spending time with the student to build trusting relationships followed—giving Harrison the increased intervention support that he desperately needed.

Leaders must be skilled in bringing parents alongside them in supporting the mental health and safety of their children. There are extenuating forces and variables that must be dealt with on a daily basis in order to maintain safety within schools. Mental health specialists and providers must no longer be viewed as a luxury in the school setting, but as a mandated and funded necessity. Supporting students with challenges, while keeping each and every student safe on campus, is imperative, and this is only possible when we have the right mental health supports and personnel working together on school teams. Youth mental health training needs to be required for all members of the school staff and offered to families annually in the school setting.

CHAPTER SUMMARY

A second grader loses self-control and injures a classmate. As the principal and her staff jump to action, and the parents are called, the reality of having crisis-management plans in place and increased mental-health support for students is apparent.

QUESTIONS FOR REFLECTION

1. How do we support students experiencing a mental health crisis while protecting the other students in our schools?
2. How do we engage families in the school safety process, provide them with education about mental health, and co-create viable safety plans with them?
3. What are ways we can better serve our students with severe mental and behavior problems and ensure teachers have the strategies and resources needed to support these students?

Chapter 12

The Power of a Trusting Relationship

Carrie Ballinger

You can't put a price tag on the life of a child.

Relationships, relationships, relationships. Mrs. Land, a seasoned educator and third-year superintendent, knew very well the vital role that building strong relationships with both staff and students plays in student success. However, she had no idea that her ability to forge a trusting relationship would mean life or death on this particular day.

As she entered the middle school campus to attend a routine meeting with a building principal, the young superintendent was passed at a high rate of speed by two city police cars, entering the school property with lights flashing and sirens blaring. A cryptic text message was delivered to her phone from the school's safety coordinator, stating that 911 had been called from within the school requesting police presence, but there was no other information known at that time. Mrs. Land's only thought was, "Those are my students, and I am responsible for their safety." She immediately knew that she must enter the school.

The CEO of the school district, ignoring thoughts to stay back at a safe distance, entered the school building at a dead run—behind two school district SROs and not having any idea of the scenario that was unfolding within the school. Was there an angry parent? Was there an intruder within the walls of the school? Had a student assaulted an adult? Had students gotten into a fight? She dared not to believe the possibility that there could be an active shooter within her middle school.

As Mrs. Land passed through the double door threshold of the building, she looked behind her to see four parents following her. She quickly shouted for them to wait in their car as the school was on lockdown. With no time for further explanation, she entered the foyer of the school and was met by an assistant principal who did not know the location from which the 911 call was made. Mrs. Land immediately instructed him to place the school on lockdown, shouting for students and staff to get to their safe place as she chased after the two police officers who were combing the school for the source of the emergency.

With an unknown situation in front of her, Mrs. Land felt defenseless as she followed behind the trained police officers empty-handed. Thoughts were running through her mind of how she could defend herself if she came face to face with an armed intruder. With all senses elevated and heart pounding, she began to look around for an item that she could use as a tool to defend herself if the situation escalated. As she and the officers passed the janitor's closet, Mrs. Land quickly grabbed the only item in sight that might provide assistance . . . a broom.

As the trio rounded the corner of the cafeteria, they heard a teacher loudly shout, "They are in the gym." The lead officer shouted back, "Who is in the gym?" The teacher approached and frantically explained that a female student had physically attacked the principal. She currently had a rope around her neck and was threatening to jump off the balcony of the gym. With her heart pounding and hands shaking, Mrs. Land followed the police officers into the gym. Her eyes immediately went to the balcony, where she saw a very familiar student. Her eyes locked with a troubled young lady who she had been mentoring for several weeks. She shook as she saw the unimaginable: her student standing with a rope around her neck and tears flowing down her face.

Mrs. Land knew immediately that she was the only person in that gym that could de-escalate the situation and ensure the child's safety. "Lord, give me the right words to say," she mumbled under her breath. Quickly, she ordered the staff present in the gym to get medical attention for the injured principal and for everyone including the police to leave the gym.

Their executive supervisor, the superintendent, was met with immediate pushback from both the staff and the police. "Look what she did to Mr. Jones! There is no way we are leaving you here alone with this student. She could hurt you, bad." With a calm that had to come from a higher being, Mrs. Land reassured her staff and the police that the student would listen to her. Ignoring the protests, she began ascending the steps to the balcony, looking back over her shoulder and whispering, "get out" to the others.

Upon reaching the top of the steps and seeing the broken chairs, flipped tables, and crushed athletic equipment, Mrs. Land quickly realized the danger she could potentially be in, but had confidence in her relationship with the student and knew she was her lifeline. In a soft whisper, she approached the student, asking her if it was okay if she sat down beside her. With an unsteady voice, the student answered, "Yes." The next words out of her mouth shook to the core, confirming her decision to approach the student alone. "Thank you for coming. I don't really want to die, but I am going to be in so much trouble. There is no other way out."

Lovingly, the superintendent looked the student in the eye and whispered, "Even when we make bad decisions, there is always hope, and there is always a way out." In a nonthreatening manner, Mrs. Land sat on the ground next to the student and invited her to sit down next to her. With the rope still pulled tightly around her neck, the student knelt but refused to sit. Ignoring the rope, Mrs. Land began to engage the student in a conversation about her favorite sport, basketball. As several minutes passed and the conversation shifted to why the student became so angry, she began to relax and sat next to Mrs. Land on the balcony floor.

As she saw that the student was beginning to relax, the courageous superintendent gently reached over and peeled the student's fingers from around the rope. Making certain to move slowly and methodically, Mrs. Land removed the rope from the student's neck as tears spilled from the student's eyes and flowed down her face. Sobbing, she shared, "I am so sorry that I hurt Mr. Jones. I got so angry, and I can't control my anger when I get that mad. Am I going to be sent to juvenile detention?" Mrs. Land embraced the student and explained to her that she would have to go to the police station and that it would be up to a judge to determine the consequences of her actions, but that she would be there to guide and support her every step of the way.

As the student cried, she and her superintendent (and caring mentor) walked hand in hand to the back door of the gym and got in the back seat of the police car, together. Mrs. Land quietly whispered a prayer of thanks for the child's safety, knowing that without her relationship with this student, the outcome could have been very different.

CHAPTER SUMMARY

As she approaches the middle school for a meeting, a school superintendent is alerted that a crisis is unfolding inside the school. What she does next is a model of discerning and caring leadership.

QUESTIONS FOR REFLECTION

1. Define the word "trust." How is trust vital in developing student relationships?
2. How do you demonstrate to students and to staff that you are worthy of their trust?
3. How has having a strong relationship with a student allowed you to peacefully de-escalate a situation?

Chapter 13

Leadership Practices for Success in Crisis Situations

Kevin Hub

> *Effective leadership requires seeing beyond the sheltered world of the local organization.*

Fortunately, most school leaders have never experienced a crisis where their leadership decisions directly impacted life or death. Nonetheless, leaders should constantly examine their thoughts on leadership and management, with the realization that what worked in the past may not work in the future. Leadership success involves embracing new paradigms and shattering old ways of thinking. School and district leaders owe it to those they lead to have a proactive vision of school safety and an arsenal of leadership practices for success in crisis situations.

BUILD THE TEAM

Successful leaders build the team. Leaders are naturally more comfortable in the company of people like them, but they should avoid the instinct to surround themselves with people having the same characteristics and leadership aptitudes as they do. Productive tension results when team members see issues uniquely and approach issues differently. When building the team, leaders should consider their own skills and then train others to complement those skills. Successful leaders in crisis situations need well-rounded teams of individuals with specific talents.

SCENARIO

An example of effective teamwork regarding a safety issue occurred when a school bus was side swiped by another vehicle. The car's mirror was ripped off, several windows were shattered, and the substitute bus driver and students on the bus were terrified. Upon hearing the news of the bus crash, the superintendent's team immediately acted.

The assistant superintendent for operations drove to the scene with the superintendent. During the drive the superintendent made several phone calls to the school principal and his communications director. The director of maintenance contacted police, fire, and EMS. He also arranged for the school bus to be staged at the nearest fire station, just two miles from the crash site. The director of communications helped the principal craft a message for her school community and also called the media to set up an interview site at the fire station where the bus would be staged. Finally, the superintendent's secretary contacted each board member and made them aware.

With a police escort, the damaged bus was driven to the fire station where another bus and driver were waiting. After checking for injuries, the students were loaded onto the new bus and taken to their homes. The individual members of the superintendent's team worked independently of one another to collectively address a serious safety incident involving many moving parts.

LEAD BY EXAMPLE

Another leadership practice is leading by example. Education leaders accept the burden of being public servants and role models. Their conduct is constantly scrutinized, so it is imperative to set the right expectations before trying to lead by example. If expectations are not clearly communicated from the beginning, then followers will develop expectations based on their perception of the example set by the leader. The best leaders set expectations first, and then lead by example.

Leading by example provides an opportunity to inspire those who follow. For some people, no matter what you do to inspire them, they will never be motivated to perform. Presence, charisma, and a few encouraging words are never enough on their own to motivate staff. Individuals typically motivate themselves, either intrinsically or extrinsically. Therefore, successful leaders in crisis situations will inspire those they lead, rather than simply motivate them.

SCENARIO

Strong leaders have a calming effect, especially during crisis situations. Just before dinner on Tuesday afternoon, the superintendent received a phone call from her high school principal. The principal discussed rumors that one of his students was telling others of plans to bring a gun to school the next day. The principal and his team did as they were trained. The team contacted law enforcement, which conducted a search of the student's home. The team conducted interviews with several students and teachers. Together, with their law enforcement partners, they concluded the threat was not credible. The superintendent agreed and made no plans to cancel school the next day.

Throughout Tuesday evening, social media was buzzing with rumors of the alleged school shooting. Local police responded with a social media post explaining the threat was not credible and that additional police would be present at school the next day as a precautionary measure.

Leading by example and inspiring confidence in her students and staff, the superintendent arrived at the high school early the next morning. She confidently walked the halls talking with teachers and staff, explaining to anyone that asked why she was sure that having school that day was the right decision. When students started arriving, she and her principal were posted confidently on the sidewalk where the car riders were dropped off by their parents. The superintendent greeted students and their parents and by her presence alone, inspired confidence that school was a safe place that day.

MAKE DECISIONS

Leaders always embracing consensus as a decision-making factor are doomed to failure. Consensus building takes forever and must be reinforced daily. Instead, effective leaders support such alternatives by using best practices, clear and direct communication, allowing patterns to emerge, and encouraging dissent when making decisions. In crisis situations, effective leaders know to weigh all the known variables and make the best decision possible. Waiting for certainty is not always possible, since delaying a decision could result in greater tragedy.

SCENARIO

On a crisp, fall morning, the director of finance and the director of maintenance came into the superintendent's office. They shared news of a

$3.7 million check that was issued and deposited, but not by the construction company for which it was intended. The superintendent decided this bizarre circumstance needed his immediate attention. Documents were examined. Interviews were conducted. It was decided that neither district employees nor the construction company were at fault.

The superintendent called the state police and FBI. In his discussions with law enforcement, they determined this was likely a case of cyber theft, and an aggressive communication effort could help recover the money before it landed overseas. Not for a second did the superintendent consider how this alleged cyber theft might reflect his reputation as a leader.

The superintendent directed his communications director to setup a press conference later that morning. He wanted to be sure the story made the noon news. In the meantime, he contacted the school board, their insurance carrier, and the local bank. The press conference ensured local coverage on the news at noon. The issue became a regional and national story later that evening. Two days later the FBI located the stolen funds in a Philadelphia branch of the local bank. The FBI credited the superintendent's decisive leadership as the reason why they were able to recover the money before it was wired overseas.

MONITOR PROGRESS

The very best leaders monitor progress. "What gets monitored gets done. Inspect what you expect." Following through on promises and commitments shows respect to the people that leaders serve. When progress is monitored, vision and action coincide to create measurable success. Before leaders can dedicate precious time necessary to monitor progress, they must prepare others to accomplish tasks critical to organizational success.

SCENARIO

Despite effective leadership, not every crisis is handled perfectly. In one district, it was common for the maintenance director to meet with each school principal during the summer to show them where the water, electric, and gas shutoffs were located. The maintenance director would escort the principal, assistant principal, and head custodian to each shutoff location in the building and demonstrate how each shutoff worked. He would watch as each person from the school leadership team engaged the shutoff mechanism.

This exercise was practiced with every principal, every summer—no matter their experience in the building. This was an accountability measure, an effort to monitor the progress of physical plant safety initiatives.

A few months into the school year, the flush mechanism on a urinal broke and water was gushing everywhere. The school principal was in a nearby hall, heard the commotion, and quickly rushed the students back to their classrooms. But, in the stress of the moment, she failed to address the problem—the water gushing from the urinal. In the few short minutes that it took the head custodian to shut off the water, it had spread into two classroom hallways, into half of the media center, and onto a four hundred square foot section of the basketball gym floor. Despite leadership efforts to practice handling physical plant crises, this principal failed to act, and the result was an insurance claim of nearly $100,000.

CHAPTER SUMMARY

Today's education leaders cannot be prepared for every school crisis. What they can do is home in on a few leadership practices to prepare them and those they lead for what might happen in the future. In this chapter, four leadership practices were examined through the lens of real-life crises.

QUESTIONS FOR REFLECTION

Build the Team

1. How can you identify smart, talented team members and provide them opportunities for influence and leadership?
2. Which skills are necessary for success in your organization?
3. What do you do to provide aspiring leaders the opportunity to gain skills necessary for leadership?

Lead by Example

1. How can educators emerge as leaders rather than managers?
2. How do you make sure others know that you value diversity?
3. What have you done to hone your leadership presence?

Make Decisions

1. How do leaders remain focused on creating positive change in the face of uncertainty, ignorance, fear, and lack of opportunity?
2. When you have made decisions based on intuition rather than logic, have you been successful? Describe a specific instance.

Monitor Progress
1. How do you examine the balance between developing others and doing things yourself?
2. How do you provide yourself and others enough time to effectively monitor progress?

Chapter 14

Keep Everyone Safe

Michael W. Kessinger

> *Accidents are not planned, and they often happen in the most unusual circumstances. The law of averages will catch up with a school that is not focused on preventive safety.*

With the many school tragedies that have occurred in the 2020s, when thinking "school safety," possible thoughts that come to a person's mind are shootings, locked school doors, security checks before one can enter the building, school resource officers walking the hallways, and even metal detectors at the front door. For some schools, there is even bulletproof glass at the main entrance.

The recent unfortunate events have resulted in our schools fostering a more secure environment for the safety of students and employees. No longer is the front door of the school left open for visitors; an ID card has to be presented for admittance. Parents cannot just walk to their child's classroom as in the past. All visitors have to be checked and signed in.

But when we talk about school safety, it has to go beyond locked doors, bulletproof windows, security guards, and monitoring who enters the building. We also have to look at how our employees work and if they are doing it in a safe environment.

A WORST-CASE SCENARIO

Mr. Tom Johnson had been principal at Central Middle School since the building was built in 2013. The school was a magnificent showplace—with inviting classrooms, auditorium, a large gymnasium, and staff who took pride in their work. There had not been a single injury on the job for any employee. It seemed like all employees followed good work practices and were careful in their daily routines.

The district's facility manager had requested a full-service health survey from KYSafe Occupational Safety and Health (KYSafe, 2022). The purpose of the consultation survey was to identify any health hazards at the school. The survey focused on the equipment, chemicals, and work processes of all schools within the district. Specific locations covered by the review were classrooms, offices, gymnasium, some of the maintenance storage, and kitchen facilities. Particular attention was given to written documentation, programs, and chemicals used on site. In addition to an inspection, interviews were conducted with employees to determine their concerns and knowledge related to safety and health issues.

Mr. Johnson had a scheduled meeting with David Peterson, consultant from the KY-OSH to review the findings from the observations and interviews, and to learn what needed to be done in the future.

"Well, Mr. Johnson, I appreciate you meeting with me today."

"Please, Mr. Peterson, call me Tom."

"And Tom, you can call me David. During the time I was here, I had the opportunity of going through your school and visiting various parts of the plant—the kitchen, maintenance room, classrooms, offices, and your outdoor HVAC unit, along with talking to your employees. We found some things that I want to go over with you to help be proactive in hopefully preventing any employee from getting injured and even avoid injuries to students."

"Well, David, I'm a little shocked. I thought our school was in pretty good shape. I do walk around and make sure that jobs are being done the way they need to be. I even make sure that no teachers are standing on chairs to hang up stuff on their bulletin boards." Tom smiled as he recently had to tell his art teacher to get a ladder instead of using a chair to hang up a student's painting.

"Tom don't get me wrong. It is good overall, but we did find some things. And, since this was a voluntary inspection, there's no fines or anything; but there are items that will need to be corrected, and you will have to write up a corrective action plan. I will tell you up front that if this had been an inspection because of a job-related injury, the things we found would have resulted in about an $88,000 fine."

"Eighty-eight thousand dollars? Are you kidding me? You found that much?" Tom was shocked. The sounds of a fine for his school made him wonder just how bad other schools were, or if his school was the worst. But he was not worrying right now about the other schools, just his own. Evidently, things were not as safe as he thought.

Overview of OSHA

The Occupational Safety and Health Administration (OSHA) is responsible to "ensure safe and healthful working conditions for workers by setting and enforcing standards and by providing training, outreach, education and assistance," (United States Department of Labor, n.d.-a, para. 1) Each state has its version of the federal OSHA. For Kentucky, KY-OSH falls under the Kentucky Education and Labor Cabinet, Department of Workplace Standards. School districts can request a voluntary survey of their schools at no cost (KYSafe, 2022).

The purpose of the survey is to identify any "imminent danger," "serious," and "other-than-serious" hazards.

- "Imminent danger" hazards are those that can "mean any conditions or practices in any place of employment which are such that a danger exists which could reasonably be expected to cause death or serious physical harm, either immediately or before the danger can be eliminated." (Missouri Department of Labor, 2021, para. 2).
- *A "serious" hazard is one that is likely "to cause serious injury, illness, or death and would be cited as a standards violation by the federal Occupational Safety and Health Administration (OSHA)." (Missouri Department of Labor, 2021, para. 3).*
- *And "other-than-serious" hazards "are cited in situations where the accident/incident or Illness that would be most likely to result from a hazardous condition would probably not cause death or serious physical harm but would have a direct and immediate relationship to the safety and health of employees" (Missouri Department of Labor, 2021, para. 4).*
- *Once the district receives the final report, it is responsible to develop a corrective action plan to address the imminent, serious, and other-than-serious hazards identified in the report for each of the schools. Typically, the report is reviewed at the district level, but as a courtesy, the building principal also has a meeting.*

"Well, Tom, we did find a few things. So, let me start. We found bleach in various locations—the janitor's room, kitchen, and the science classroom."

"Wait, you found bleach? We don't even order bleach. I can understand maybe a little bleach in the kitchen where they have the washing machine to wash their cleaning cloths. But not in the janitor's room. How did it get there?"

"Evidently, Tom, you have a janitor who personally purchased the bleach to help with cleaning and disinfecting. I mean, she spent her own money on it. At least that's what she told me. She really wants to do a good job, and she says that sometimes the materials she thinks are needed are not purchased. You know how some of these older ladies are. They are 'old school,' and bleach is sometimes their answer to cleaning challenges. All we're trying to do here is make sure that we keep everyone safe. That's it. Just keep everyone safe."

FLASHBACK TO 1991

Keep everyone safe. Keep everyone safe. Tom's mind went back to the first school he served as principal in the district. That phrase, *keep everyone safe*, reminded him of a conversation he had with Gary Smith, the district's manager of district-wide services and the district's asbestos designee. The high school Tom first served as principal was an old school built in the early 1960s. And Gary was there on Tom's first week on the job to go over some things with him so he would be aware of the big picture and the various nuances of the school.

"So, Tom, it's great to have you back in the district, and I can't believe you're starting as the principal. Just seems like it was yesterday that you were a student here when I was principal."

"Yes, Mr. Smith. I remember when you were my principal, and you were a good one. So, I hope I can follow in your footsteps and do just as good of a job as you did."

"Well thank you, Tom. That is very nice of you to say. But let's talk a bit about why I'm here today. This school is an old school, and it has some potential issues with it. One of the things I need to talk to you about is something which we just became aware of. We have both confirmed and assumed asbestos in the building."

"Asbestos! I thought that was illegal to use in school buildings. Where is this asbestos located or assumed to be?"

"Tom, we haven't added any asbestos to this building, but we had to get an inspection and a report for OSHA. The AHERA regulation required all schools to be inspected. See that notebook over there on the shelf? That is the report for this school. Didn't they teach you anything in your principal courses about asbestos?"

Asbestos Hazard Emergency Response Act (AHERA)

Enacted in 1986, the Asbestos Hazard Emergency Response Act provided procedures to address asbestos in school buildings. Typically, prior to 1980, asbestos containing materials (ACM) were used in schools to provide a degree of fire protection, insulation, and sound reduction (Ellis & Foster, 2023). Places where ACM might exist in schools are in ceiling tile, floor tile and the glue to hold it down, boilers, furnace, pipe wrapping, insulation in walls and ceiling, textured walls and ceilings, sheetrock, and even in some school supplies such as chalk and crayons.

After the passing of AHERA, schools have their buildings inspected by a certified asbestos inspector. The inspection determined if and where ACM were present by obtaining a number of samples and having those samples tested by an accredited lab. If sampling was not possible as it would disturb the area, then the area (for example, ceiling insulation) would be assumed to be ACM. Once inspections were completed, then a management plan was developed by a certified asbestos management planner.

AHERA requires a yearly notification to parents, teachers, and even employee organizations on the availability of the management plan. Also, notification must be provided if any asbestos related action will be occurring. Reinspections are required every three years by a certified inspector, and an update to the plan also occurs. In addition to inspections, reinspections, and annual notifications, training of custodial staff is to occur annually, so the staff are aware of how to properly maintain ACM.

The Kentucky Department of Education (KDE), Division of District Support annually collects information from districts regarding their facilities. The inventory and classified system are used by KDE to "access their K–12 public school buildings" physical condition and educational suitability in a standardized, fair, and equitable manner" (Kentucky Department of Education, 2023-a, para. 1).

On their website, KDE reports the condition of the school currently in operation. In addition, the year the facility was built is also provided. Out of the 1046 facilities reported by districts and presented on the Unofficial State Report of Kentucky Facilities, 625 (59.75 percent) of the facilities were built prior to 1980 (KDE, 2023). While many have had additions and renovations completed, one might assume that the complete abatement of any ACM most likely did not occur due to cost. If you visit a building that has been around for more than four decades, more than likely you will find a very common ACM in the floor tile.

"Tom, look down at your feet. There are nine by nine floor tiles throughout this building. Those floor tiles contain asbestos. And even the mastic, the glue, has asbestos fibers in it. We can't just remove them. We have to maintain and not do any crazy things.

"You have some new janitors here and I'm going to cover this with them, but I want you to also know that they cannot just go and dry buff the tiles. If you dry buff the floor tiles, then some asbestos dust could be released. The janitors have to make sure the floors are somewhat covered with liquid whenever they buff them. That's really the most important thing. No dry buffing. No dry polishing the wax. Oh, that is another important thing. Keep the floors waxed. That will help to capsulate the asbestos.

"And then the ceiling tiles—those are old ceiling tiles, and some of them have asbestos in them. We only had a few of them tested, so we just assume every one of the ceiling tiles in the school contains asbestos. You remember how you boys threw your pencils up to stick them in the ceiling. Well, that can't happen because when you throw the pencil up there and it sticks, once you pull it out it can release some of the fibers. We're hoping we can eventually replace all the ceiling tiles in the school, but that's very expensive. So right now, we just ask that you don't join the students to see who can stick the most pencils in the ceiling. I think you were the champ back in the day.

"And then we have steam pipes–the wrapping around them. That wrap around the pipes also has asbestos in it. What we do is paint over those to encapsulate the asbestos. It's a pain, but it's what we need to do because we can't do an abatement. That would cost us hundreds of thousands of dollars. When you get a moment, you might want to take a look at those notebooks over there. They will tell you where we think all the asbestos is and what you need to do to maintain it in safe condition. Remember all we're trying to do is to keep everyone safe." Keep everyone safe.

BACK TO THE PRESENT

What a memory! When I started it was asbestos, now it is bleach. What is the problem with bleach?

"So, David, what is the problem with bleach?"

"It's not just the bleach, Tom, there are other corrosive liquids I found. There's the corrosive bleach, Array Ultimate Sanitizer, Liquid Swabby II, and Lysol Ultimate Toilet Bowl Cleaner in the janitor and kitchen areas, and corrosive bleach and corrosive chemicals in the science classrooms. It's that you also don't have any suitable emergency eyewashes for employees to use. There is a need for eyewash and safety shower equipment to be installed. I also saw that your teachers, cooks, and janitors don't wear eye shields or aren't wearing gloves when they use those chemicals. You do have PPE materials here, don't you? And where is the documented training you provided to anyone using these corrosive materials?"

"PPE?" Tom had heard that term before, but in his recent finance class, PPE meant per-pupil expenditures—the amount of money, on average, being spent by the district per student.

"Personal protective equipment. I'm talking about gloves, face shields, protective eyewear, anything that would protect the employee, or students in a lab setting. And also, in a place where bleach or another chemical could in someone's eyes, there needs to be a way of washing it out, so, an eye rinse station."

"Now, Tom, we not only saw bleach, but we also saw the toilet bowl cleaner. And the toilet bowl cleaner has a form of acid in it. Again, if that acid or the toilet bowl cleaner happened to get on people's hands or splash into their faces, there could be a real big issue with worker's compensation. What we're trying to do is make sure that your employees are safe and that the district doesn't have a big worker's comp claim.

"And to make sure students don't get into the bleach and corrosive chemicals, they need to be secured. In fact, they need to be in a locked cabinet because they are dangerous. Now I know your students aren't going to go and drink anything, but we know how middle school students are, and we just want to make sure that we don't have an incident.

"There's a couple of other things we found that we need to talk about, Tom. I found some spray bottles that were not labeled or marked with the content. Those spray bottles must have an identification of what's in them. We don't want someone to just grab a bottle, assume it's one thing, and it be something else. All containers must be properly marked.

"There also is not a master list of hazardous chemicals at the school. This list should have the name of the substance as reported on the container's label. This list should be a location either in the janitor's room, or even the front office. The idea here is if something were to happen, the list of hazardous chemicals can easily be provided to medical personnel and to our office.

"I mentioned earlier about training documentation. There needs to be documentation of training that has been provided to your workers. If it's been done, I'll need a copy of it. If there is no documentation, then we need to start doing it.

"So, with the various corrosive materials, the lack of employees using PPE and really some limitation as to what PPE you have available, the unlabeled spray bottles, no list of chemicals on the premise, and the lack of documented training, if this were to have been a real inspection, there would be fine of around $88,000. But we're glad that it wasn't.

"You will be receiving a written report in seven to ten days. If you have any questions, please call me, and I'll make a trip here to talk more about the report. You will have to do a corrective action plan, and there are some forms you will need to complete. And you have 120 days to get that to me, so no big rush. There are things you can do now such as addressing the PPE issue, labeling those spray bottles and starting to get that inventory list created. And also, don't forget about training your employees. There will be more about that in the report you will receive.

"Any questions, Tom?"

At that moment, the phone rang. "Excuse me a second, David."

The secretary was on the other end of the phone. "Mr. Johnson, I'm so sorry to bother you, but I have two students sitting in here. They were brought by the PE teacher. They were fighting, again, in class."

"Thank you, Mary. I'll be right out."

Hanging up the phone, Tom turned his attention back to the issue at hand. "No, David. No questions right now, but I'm sure I will. Thank you. Got to take care of two students now who got into a fight. Got to keep them safe."

CHAPTER SUMMARY

A principal receives a friendly "off the record" visit that identifies several OSHA violations in his building. He is reminded that school safety goes far beyond keeping out unwanted intruders.

QUESTIONS FOR REFLECTION

1. How have your faculty and staff been trained on the proper use of chemicals they might use in the performance of their duties and in the classroom?
2. How does the actions of your faculty and staff ensure they are being safe in performing their daily routines?
3. When was the last time, if applicable, you looked at the school's asbestos inspection report?
4. What are the other areas the administration, faculty, and staff need to consider when attempting to keep everyone safe?

REFERENCES

Ellis, M. W., & Foster, D. (2023). School buildings, teachers, and asbestos exposure. Retrieved March 8, 2023 from https://mesothelioma.net/school-buildings-teachers-asbestos-exposure/Kentucky Department of Education (KDE). (2023-a). *Kentucky facilities inventory and classification system.*

Kentucky Department of Education (KDE). (2023). *Updated unofficial state report.* Retrieved on February 8, 2023 from https://education.ky.gov/districts/fac/Pages/Kentucky%20Facilities%20Inventory%20and%20Classification%20System.aspx

KYSafe. (2022). *Consultative*. Retrieved March 10, 2023 from https://kysafe.ky.gov/services/Pages/consult.aspx

Missouri Department of Labor. (2021). *What is an imminent danger condition, a serious or other-than-serious hazard?* Retrieved March 10, 2023 from https://laboranswers.mo.gov/hc/en-us/articles/4405252992535-What-is-an-imminent-danger-condition-a-serious-or-other-than-serious-hazard-United States Department of Labor. (n.d.). *Occupational Safety and Health Administrations: About OSHA*. Retrieved March 10, 2023 from https://www.osha.gov/about osha

Chapter 15

Baby Bear Wants His Porridge ... Now!

Franklin Thomas

> *Perfection is not attainable, but if we chase perfection, we can catch excellence.*—Vince Lombardi

It was late September of 2001, and Matthew was serving as a first-year high school assistant principal. The nation, still reeling from the September 11 attacks, was in the midst of the anthrax attacks. These attacks targeted six news outlets and two U.S. senators with letters laced with anthrax. Matthew was conducting a classroom observation of a teacher when another teacher, David, interrupted and asked him to step into the hallway.

David shared that he had just opened a letter received by the school by running his fingers underneath the flap, and now his fingers were burning and a little red. He was concerned that the letter may have contained anthrax. Matthew asked who had sent the letter, and David replied that it was from a familiar textbook publishing company. Matthew reassured him that he had probably just irritated his fingers a bit when opening the letter and that he should wash his hands and that he would be fine.

Matthew returned to the classroom, finished his observation, and went to the principal's office to file the observation. When he entered the office, he found David reporting his concern about the letter to the principal. The principal indicated that she was going to call the district office and report what had happened. Matthew justified his position that there should be no concern by pointing out that the anthrax attacks were very few, directed at well-known news organizations and legislators, the letter was from a familiar and reputable source, and that there was a plausible explanation for his fingers being irritated. Nevertheless, the principal proceeded to call the district office.

As the call was taking place, Matthew said out loud, "You're making a mistake."

A debacle ensued. David had opened the letter while in a classroom full of students. He and all of those students were quarantined until well after school was dismissed, in order to be assessed by medical professionals. The remaining students were required to walk to a nearby middle school where they were housed in the gym until school was dismissed. Several government agencies were contacted for assistance. News outlets descended with huge trucks with satellite dishes. The decision was made to cancel school in the entire district the following day until the situation was sorted out.

The following day, the conclusion was reached that there was no anthrax involved and that David had simply irritated his fingers due to the manner in which he opened the envelope. You may recall that this is the exact explanation that Matthew formulated when David first raised his concern. This is an example of a complete *overreaction*.

So, what was the harm of erring on the side of caution? Hundreds of kids and their parents were frightened. The school day was disrupted. The planned school calendar was disrupted. Resources were routed to an incident that should not have been an incident. And those seeking to terrorize America succeeded in winning that battle in Matthew's school system without even trying. This happened in a school system that prided itself on having had school on September 12, 2001, while many were canceling, so that the terrorists wouldn't be winning in their school system.

Fast forward sixteen years and Matthew is now an assistant superintendent. Once again, he is going about his business when the superintendent walks into his office and says that one of the elementary school principals has called and needs assistance with a disgruntled parent. The two drive to the school, which is about fifteen minutes away. When they arrive, they proceed to the principal's office to get briefed on the issue. When they enter, the superintendent notices a big box of assorted donuts. He asks if he can have one and then begins to partake. A bit of small talk ensues and then Matthew and the superintendent are informed that the parent is currently waiting in a conference room and that she is very angry at one of the teachers.

Suddenly, a teacher bursts through the office door in tears. She is the teacher with whom the parent is angry. The parent was left to wait for an extended period of time, unattended in the conference room. This was not only a bad idea, but also made the parent even more angry. She finally decided to take matters into her own hands and went to the teacher's classroom and confronted her in front of her class of second graders. The parent then left through a side door. Not having someone stay with the parent in the conference room, perhaps someone who could talk to them and calm them down, and enjoying a donut before dealing with a serious issue is an example of complete *underreaction*.

So, what was the harm? In this case, it was a room full of second graders frightened by a strange woman invading their classroom and yelling at their teacher. It was also a teacher who had to be the object of the yelling followed by feeling unsupported by her superintendent who was eating a donut instead of dealing with a serious situation. But it could have been so much worse. What if the parent had physically attacked the teacher? What if she had been armed? What if she had been angry about something that one of the other students had done to her child and attacked that student?

The first sentence of the title of this chapter should now begin to make sense. "Baby bear likes his porridge not too hot and not too cold, but just right." Likewise, school officials need to make their responses to school safety issues not too hot (an overreaction) and not too cold (an underreaction), but just right. That sounds hard. However, the good news is that sometimes school officials have plenty of time to consider their reactions and consult with others.

An example might be a severe storm being predicted for the day after tomorrow. What precautions should be taken? Would it be better to just cancel school? The bad news is that sometimes school officials have mere seconds to determine their reactions. An example might be a teacher calls the school office saying that a student burned themselves in chemistry class, and now, the last word of the title of this chapter makes sense. The porridge needs to be just right . . . now!

How do you prepare to get your level of reaction perfect every time?

- Foremost, you have to realize that you will not get it perfect every time. However, you can increase your chances of success by having detailed plans in place for common school safety incidents. Such planning can effectively take care of one of those situations that requires an immediate response and also provide the luxury of getting to consider a response carefully and collaborate with others.
- Another strategy is to practice formulating a response to situations. This can be in the form of staged and announced events like active shooter drills but could also take the form of "tabletop" exercises. Imagine reading one of the school safety issues described in this book to your school safety team and then asking them to formulate a response in one minute, and then give them another try, allowing thirty minutes.
- Lastly, you must learn from your mistakes (and good decisions) by carefully debriefing each actual school safety incident with your team. This can make something good come from a misstep.

CHAPTER SUMMARY

School officials are reminded that there can be overreaction and underreaction to school safety incidents. Proactive planning can prevent such missteps, and strategies are offered to help achieve a balance.

QUESTIONS FOR REFLECTION

1. Describe a time when you have known of a school safety team overreacting.
   a. What harm resulted?
   b. What lessons were learned?
   c. How could the overreaction have possibly been prevented?
2. Describe a time when you have known of a school safety team underreacting.
   a. What harm resulted?
   b. What lessons were learned?
   c. How could the underreaction have possibly been prevented?

REFERENCES

Borum, R., Cornell, D. G., Modzeleski, W., & Jimerson, S. R. (2010). What can be done about school shootings?: A review of the evidence. *Educational Researcher, 39*(1), 27–37. https://doi.org/10.3102/0013189X09357620

Bradshaw, C. P., Debnam, K. J., Kush, J. M., & Johnson, S. L. (2022). Planning for a crisis, but preparing for every day: What predicts schools' preparedness to respond to a school safety crisis? *Frontiers in Communication, 7*, 1–5. https://doi.org/10.3389/fcomm.2022.765336

Madfis, E. (2016). "It's better to overreact": School officials' fear and perceived risk of rampage attacks and the criminalization of American public schools. *Critical Criminology 24*, 39–55. https://doi.org/10.1007/s10612-015-9297-0

Maor, M. (2012). Policy overreaction. *Journal of Public Policy, 32*(3), 231–59. doi:10.1017/S0143814X1200013X

Chapter 16

Bad Decisions Can Be Made with the Best of Intentions

Rebecca Howell

> *Without consistent rules and healthy boundaries, the life of a child and the culture of a school can soon become chaos.*

Cindy was reaching the end of a normal school day in the life of a principal. She read her email one last time before she began her afternoon dismissal routine. She would mark her bus lists for absences, grab the bus radio, and proceed to the gym to wait on students to check in with her before they boarded buses. The gym was set up for the annual ABC Fashion Show, performed for the kindergarten classes each year. The stage was set, as her school always converted their chorus risers into a runway—and the kids loved it.

One can imagine the curiosity the kids had upon entering the gym for buses that day. All of their eyes lit up when they entered. The bleachers that were normally down were flipped on their sides directly behind the stage and were strategically positioned to allow the curtain to be closed to hide them. Cindy knew the arrangement in the gym would cause the kids to be extra wild. She had to tell many students they could not walk on the stage.

The gym continued to fill up with students, and the excitement grew. Eventually, Mrs. Moore made her way to the gym with her five students and several assistants. She was a resource teacher for a behavior unit. She had the highest number of exceptional students in the entire school, and Jake was one of them. He had only been at Cindy's school for a few weeks, and it had been a rough transition.

Many days had been spent on modifying Jake's behavior. He was violent with teachers, staff, and kids, and had been restrained or confined multiple times. But, when he was not escalated, he was a very sweet, ten-year-old little boy. Cindy knew very well what behaviors Jake was capable of. She currently had a scab on her leg from where he had bitten her the previous week. Still, Cindy had a heart spot for him. His story was so sad. He had spent his whole life in hostile unstable environments and was currently being raised by a great aunt.

As soon as Jake saw the stage, he took off running toward it. He had been known to run from teachers before, so this made all the adults in the gym run after him. Cindy and Mrs. Moore caught him before he reached the stage. Fortunately, he stopped running and Mrs. Moore reminded him that he was not to be on the stage. Something about that stuck with Cindy. She knew she had told many children herself they couldn't be on the stage, but she couldn't help but think of all the times during the day Jake was told "no." This was such a small thing for him to ask to do.

Cindy has sixteen years of experience leading schools with behavior units. She well understood the need for boundaries, structure, and routines for students with emotional behavior disorders. She also understood why Mrs. Moore gave Jake the direction that she did, but just this once she wanted Jake to be told "yes." Cindy knew if she allowed Jake to walk the stage, other kids would see him, but she had a strong feeling that they would know why he would be allowed. They knew who the resource kids were, and they loved them.

Cindy wanted to continue to build trust with Jake, so she allowed him to walk the stage. She watched as Mrs. Moore's eyes grew wide when she heard her tell Jake he could walk the stage. She gestured towards Mrs. Moore in a way as to reassuringly say, "I got this." Truth was, Cindy had just set events in motion that could not be undone. Jake immediately took advantage of the upper hand. His walking the stage immediately turned to him climbing the bleachers that were flipped on their side. It did not take him long to reach the top and stand to his feet shouting to the kids below that he was going to jump off and fly.

Cindy watched the consequences of her decision play out in real time. She quickly scrambled to make sure there was enough staff to load the buses, so she could assist her EBD staff in trying to deescalate the situation she had caused. Jake was supposed to be loading onto his bus, but instead, he was standing high on the bleachers. After much pleading, bribing, begging, and anything else she could think of, Cindy finally had to call his great aunt to come to the school get him because he was not coming down.

Cindy, Mrs. Moore, and several staff were with Jake in the gym when his great aunt arrived at school. The buses were long gone, and the gym was empty except for the entourage that was trying to protect Jake. She walked into the gym with a huge smile on her face and laughingly said to Jake,

"Come on buddy. It's time to stop goofing off and go home. Show's over." Cindy stared in disbelief at the aunt's lack of concern over the situation. Jake immediately began walking down the bleachers, and he and his aunt giggled the whole way out the doors to their car.

At this time, all Cindy could do was apologize to Mrs. Moore about her lapse in judgment. She explained her reasoning, but this did little to make the situation any better. In fact, she understood how Jake had just won a power struggle and that alone would make Mrs. Moore's day harder with him tomorrow. Moving forward, Cindy never allowed herself to make that mistake again. She knew it was a perfect example of a bad decision made with the best of intentions.

CHAPTER SUMMARY

An experienced school principal makes a critical error in judgement by going against the decision of her teacher and allowing a student a privilege because she felt too much empathy for his situation. The event, which occurred due to her decision, escalated to an unsafe environment for everyone.

QUESTIONS FOR REFLECTION

1. Reflect upon your career as an educator. Can you think of a time when a decision that you made produced the opposite outcome of what you had hoped for?
2. During your time as an educator, have you ever allowed your empathy for a student to cloud your professional judgement with a decision that you made?
3. Moving forward, what are the negative impacts of Cindy's decision on Jake and Mrs. Moore?

REFERENCE

Wink, M. N., LaRusso, M. D., & Smith, R. L. (2021). Teacher empathy and students with problem behaviors: Examining teachers' perceptions, responses, relationships, and burnout. *Psychology in the Schools, 58*(8), 1575–96.

Chapter 17

Ready at All Costs or Ready at All?

Leslie Todd Watts

> *Every year, school administrators sacrifice substantial amounts of time and energy to ensure the safety and well-being of students. Being willing to make those sacrifices develops trust among stakeholders that can often be leveraged for future success.*

After another routine day at Euclid Elementary, Todd was getting ready to shut his computer after debriefing with his assistant principal. His assistant principal had to attend a school program for his daughter, and he had just left. It was November. The school year was in its late fall rhythm. Routines had been established and the occasional behavior issues were increasing, with it being just a few weeks before Thanksgiving break. It was a gray, dreary, and rainy Thursday afternoon. That's when Todd's cell phone rang. Karen, the transportation director, was on the phone.

"Todd, we've got a bus driver who said one of your fifth-grade students said she was going to bring a gun to school tomorrow. He didn't hear it directly, but two other students came up to him and told him she had said it."

This wasn't the first time Todd had dealt with a school threat. After all, he had worked three years as an assistant principal at the district's high school. Threats of gun violence unfortunately had become the routine rather than the exception.

"Who is the student?" Todd knew most of the school's 330 kids by name. The faces of fifth-grade students flashed through his head as he tried to think ahead.

"It's Sarah. She told her cousin, and her cousin told the older kids. Then they told the driver. She's been awful on the bus this week, Todd. Her mouth just won't stop, either."

Todd thought to himself, "Sarah? She's never had any issues." There were no behavior events listed on Infinite Campus. Every behavior had a reason. It was to get something or get out of something. At the same time, even successful students make mistakes and poor choices. He wondered what could have possibly happened to cause her to make such a statement.

What's worse, he knew inaction was not an option—Columbine, Sandy Hook, Parkland, Newport News. Through his threat assessment training, he knew one could never be certain. Everything must always be investigated. There were too many examples where administrators thought something was insignificant and the consequences were too often tragically significant. This was a chance Todd wasn't willing to take.

"Thanks, Karen. I'll call Shane, and we'll begin our threat assessment protocol. I'll keep you updated." Karen gave Todd the bus driver's number.

It was 4:50 p.m. on Thursday afternoon. The district local planning committee was meeting at 5:30 p.m. at the central office. Todd also had a family dinner scheduled at 6:30 p.m. He had a feeling those plans were about to change. He was fortunate to work in a district where the school resource officers had great relationships with the principals. He called Shane, the school resource officer (SRO), on his way to central office and briefed him on the details Karen had given him.

"Shane, we've had a threat on one of our buses. One of our fifth graders said she was going to bring a gun to school tomorrow. Right now, that's all I know. I'm going to call the bus driver and see if I can get in touch with the mom."

Like Todd, Shane didn't want to take a chance, either. "Tell you what, let's do a home visit after your meeting and see if we can prevent as much as we can here." Todd appreciated this about his SRO. Being proactive and taking the inconvenient steps to solve a problem and communicate usually led to positive outcomes.

Most administrators are taught the best practice of talking to the student first in matters concerning discipline. The problem here was that it was after school hours. The bus driver did not provide any other details. Todd tried the two numbers in Infinite Campus. There was no answer, and each call went straight to voicemail. He entered Sarah's address in his phone. He noticed two households—one with a grandmother and one with her mom. They lived about fifteen miles apart. Todd texted his wife and told her it would be another late night with a student issue. She was not surprised, as she was all too familiar with "when duty calls."

Todd met Shane and climbed into the police cruiser, and they headed toward the first address. The end of the fifteen-mile drive ended in a line of battered, white trailers. Shane flashed a light at the house numbers, looking for the one that matched Sarah's address.

"That's the one, but it doesn't look like anyone's home." No sooner had Shane said this, and a voice came out of the dark in a low tone.

"You boys need a place to stop, or are you gonna get on?" Todd swallowed and took a breath. He saw a man's silhouette come out from beside the front porch.

"I've got this, Shane," he whispered. "My name is Todd Watts, and I'm the principal at Euclid Elementary. I'm trying to find one of our students, and this is the address we have. Something happened on the bus today, and we wanted to talk to her before school tomorrow." Shane whispered to Todd to remind him, "We don't know who this is."

"You looking for Sarah? She's not here. She's with her mom at the other trailer."

"Finally," Todd thought. "We're at least getting somewhere." And he kept the conversation going.

"I don't have a working number for her mom. Is there any way you could help us get in contact with her?" The man approached the cruiser on the passenger side while Shane gently put the cruiser in gear—just in case. The man got his phone out and dialed a number.

"Hey, I've got the principal of Sarah's school here. They wanna talk to you." He handed the phone to Todd. The mom sounded a little out of it but gave Todd another address located in an adjacent county. It was about twelve miles away and not on file. Todd let her know he would be there in twenty minutes.

After another long drive, Shane and Todd found themselves at another trailer tucked into the side of a hill. It had started to rain again. As Shane pulled the cruiser into the mud driveway, Sarah's mom came out. She was wearing a sleeveless shirt and her bare feet squished in the mud.

"Ma'am, I don't want to have you out here any longer than you need to be, and we try to talk to the student first in situations like this, but I wanted to let you know that Sarah apparently told another student on the bus today that she was going to bring a gun to school tomorrow. Has she talked to you since she got home?"

"Yeah, I saw her for a second. She's at my cousin's house. She said a sixth grader was yelling at her and she didn't want to hear it anymore. But she shouldn't have said that." Her voice trailed off.

"I know this is inconvenient, but we take safety very seriously. I wanted to talk to her as well. Can you bring her to school tomorrow instead of her riding the bus?"

"Yes, that's fine. I understand, and I appreciate you coming out here and letting me know. See, the problem is some guys came to my mom's house Tuesday night, and they beat up Sarah's uncle. Last night, someone shot three holes in the side of the house where Sarah sleeps. That's why I sent her to my cousin's house. We reported it to the sheriff, and we've been up at night ever since. We don't have any guns in the house. She's been up with us, too."

"Listen, we'll talk to her as part of our threat assessment. Usually, I tell parents I want to try to prove innocence and not guilt. We also want to help Sarah get some added support."

Todd shook the mom's hand and thanked her for talking to them. *It's not supposed to be that easy*, he thought. He was used to parents at the high school putting up a fight. At least now, there was a clearer picture as to why. Every situation has a "why." It was unfortunate here, because he wondered just how much trauma Sarah had seen in the past week. She did not have access to guns, but she had certainly been impacted by the drama. Unfortunately, this is where most threat assessments and interventions stop. For Todd and his team, this is where they begin.

On the way back to school, Todd called the superintendent to update him on the situation, as well as the transportation director, letting her know Sarah would not be riding the bus the following morning. He finally made it home around 9:30 p.m. that night, but he felt like he could sleep a little more soundly because he took the necessary steps to get to the root of an issue and be in a position to provide support rather than simply administer reactive consequences.

The next morning, Todd, the assistant principal, and the guidance counselor conducted a threat assessment. Their investigation determined that Sarah made that comment because, in her words, "That sixth grader wouldn't leave me or my cousin alone. I just wanted her to stop! I don't even have a gun. I've just been wishing my uncle hadn't gotten beat up. I haven't slept very much."

The threat assessment did its job, but Todd always looked to provide support when possible. His administration team worked with Sarah's mom to set up additional wrap-around services with a check-in-check-out system and school-based counseling twice a week. As the school year continued, Sarah landed a major role in the school's spring production and had no further behavior incidents.

CHAPTER SUMMARY

An elementary school principal initiates an investigation concerning a student who has threatened to bring a gun to school the next day. Postponing an evening event with his family, he and the school resource officer track down the student's mother. Through this time-consuming investigation, the administrative team uses a threat assessment to accurately provide interventions and supports that result in a positive outcome for the student, rather than reactive consequences.

QUESTIONS FOR REFLECTION

1. What kinds of protocols/systems does your school/district have in place when dealing with school threats outside of school hours?
2. How has your school/district developed relationships with law enforcement to assist with investigations?
3. How often do you train your school-based threat assessment teams with scenarios? Are your teams ready at all costs?
4. How would you assess your threat assessment/response process?
5. If you were in Todd's position, what would you have done differently?

REFERENCE

Mirsky, L. (2011). Building safer, saner schools. *Educational Leadership, 69*(1), 45–49.

Chapter 18

We Can't Do Everything

Krystal Conway-Cunningham and Michael W. Kessinger

> *As school leaders, the safety and well-being of every one of our students is always at the forefront of our minds. Ensuring that we are providing our students with the tools they need to be successful is essential.*

It was after 3 p.m. The school bell to dismiss the students for the day had just rung. The hallways were now filled with all the eager high schoolers ready to take the trip home. Teachers were in their respective areas monitoring the hallways, as over 1,000 students made their way to their departure areas to leave school for the day. Sally was tiding up her room when she heard over the intercom: "Please excuse this interruption. All faculty and staff please report to the library for the staff meeting."

Everyone made their way into the library media center located on the first floor of the building. Sally found a seat at the table with the rest of the mathematics department. She was a bit nervous, yet open-minded about the meeting. This was her first official staff meeting as a first-year Option 6 teacher, pursuing alternate teacher certification when she realized she wanted to be a teacher after obtaining her bachelor's in chemistry and master's in environmental studies.

As the principal began his slideshow, he stated, "We have had a great couple of first days of school. You all have worked hard, and your efforts have not gone unnoticed. Thank you all for monitoring the hallways and ensuring that every student is where they need to be." As he continued to go through each slide, reviewing the upcoming events and testing that was about to start, he summarized with a segment on "borderline students." The more Sally listened to this segment of the meeting, the more she grew worried.

"For those who do not know, our borderline students are those to whom we need to give special attention. These are the ones that need an extra push to get over the finish line. These students should be graduating this year, but they are going to need our help," said the principal.

"Here is Tommy. Tommy does not have the best home life. When we can get him to focus on school, he does a great job. However, once home life starts to affect him, he goes downhill again."

"This is Jane. We all know and love her, but Jane is another one that needs help in the classroom. She understands the material but can sometimes get easily distracted. She is another student that has home life issues that affect her on a daily basis."

Student after student, it was the same story. They would do well, but then something would happen and cause the student to decline again. These kids, in Sally's mind, were on a never-ending roller coaster ride called "life." She finally got to the point that she could not take it anymore. Thinking back to her own childhood, she thought to herself, "This could have easily been me."

For Sally, life always threw her curve balls or "lemons." It was the teachers and friends' parents in her life that taught her how to make lemonade out of those lemons. The teachers, specifically, showed her that life is what we make it. They told her that even though she experienced a lot of trauma over the years, her past did not have to dictate her future. They taught her coping skills that she still uses to this day.

Sally raised her hand and waited for the principal to call on her. When he did, she said, "I am hearing that these students have experienced a lot of traumas in their lives. From how you described it, they do well until something in their lives throws them off track. It appears that they do not know how to cope with the things that throw them off track. What can we do to teach them coping skills?"

The look the principal gave her almost made Sally wish she had not said anything. However, she knew she did not say anything wrong. There were several teachers that gave her a reassuring smile and a slight nod that helped to ease her nerves.

Finally, the principal said, "We can't do everything." Then, he turned back to his slideshow and continued the meeting.

Jane knew she missed a lot of days from school. She knew she had a test coming up in Mrs. Sally's Algebra 2 class, and she had make-up assignments to complete for all her other classes.

"This is my senior year; I just want to graduate," she thought.

Jane hated missing school because school was her only refuge from the chaos at home. Since her father passed away, she knew she had to help with the bills and day-to-day functions of the house. She worked hard to keep it all balanced, but some days it felt as though she had the weight of the world on her shoulders. Her senior year was supposed to be fun. She was supposed to be hanging out with her friends and making memories. Instead, she was forced into the family business.

Jane's family was infamous for selling drugs, and other crimes just came along with the territory. Her aunts and uncles had lofty expectations for her. She was tasked with selling to the younger crowd and finding new recruits. Jane knew all of this was wrong. She had other dreams, but she felt trapped. When she tried to leave the family business the last time, she ended up in the hospital with a broken arm, a black eye, and the idea that she could never leave this lifestyle.

Jane kept her head down. At home, she did what the family told her to do. In school, she did just enough for most teachers to not ask questions. She worked hard to not be noticed.

But Mrs. Sally noticed Jane. She noticed her absences. She saw through her lies about what happened to her arm and eye. She noticed the sadness on Jane's face and the disconnection in her demeanor. Mrs. Sally paid close attention to all her students. She wanted to help Jane in any way she could. The stress she had faced as a child helped her understand that Jane needed trauma-informed care.

Thinking back to that day in the staff meeting, Sally wished she had shared her knowledge about trauma-informed education. Perhaps she could have offered some helpful practices that the teachers could have used in their classrooms or explained the triggered responses resulting from trauma in the students' lives. These students were bringing an invisible backpack every day to school, filled with all their responsibilities, the traumas they endured, and the weight of everything combined.

CHAPTER SUMMARY

A teacher remembers her own traumatic childhood and reflects on her at-risk students. She realizes she needs to make her colleagues more aware of "trauma-informed care" intervention strategies.

QUESTIONS FOR REFLECTION

1. What social-emotional, trauma-informed care protocols does your school have in place?
2. How do you provide intervention care for the at-risk students in your classroom?

3. How does your school provide proactive support for the parents of these students?

REFERENCE

Kentucky Revised Statue 158.441. (2019). SB 1 School Safety and Resiliency Act. Kentucky Department of Education. Retrieved from https://education.ky.gov/school/sdfs/Pages/School-Safety-and-Resiliency-Act-%28Senate-Bill%2C-2019%29.aspx.

Chapter 19

The Quiet Kid

Taylor Lauck and Christina Drury

The lost boys (and girls) are the students who are often likely to inflict harm on self and others. And the peril of delay is costly.

The walls of windows in each classroom brought in an abundance of sunshine and warmth. It was hard not to be in awe of the new school building. That day, however, was an oddly dreary day. The rain continued to pour as the hours passed. It was a quarter till noon, and the senior's main focus was the upcoming lunch period.

The cafeteria—oh, it was beautiful. The design offered so much seating, including an outdoor gated area with picnic tables in the back of the building. Students could look out the big paned windows and enjoy the outdoors without stepping a foot outside. The inviting entrance made it easily accessible to change one's mind about where to sit. Even with the rain, it still looked beautiful.

"Johnny, over here! I saved you a seat," said Anthony.

Hands full, Johnny came over and plopped down. "This rain makes me so tired. I about fell asleep in chemistry earlier. Just staring at the rain put me in a trance."

"At least we have not seen 'Loner Landon' today. I wonder where he is spreading misery today," said Eric.

Landon had moved here in August from Mississippi. The kid looked like he had never stepped foot in a school. He dressed normally in all black with an occasional grey, oversized hoodie. His hair never looked washed and the bags under his eyes looked like it had been days since he slept. Landon never said anything, but his cold, blank stare said what he did not verbalize.

"Hey! He is not here, so I do not care. And you know what that means? Mrs. Gem will not complain about his lack of effort today in chemistry, so it's a win all around."

Mrs. Gem never made the effort to get to know her students. What was the purpose? They came in groups of thirty and left fifty minutes later. She did not have time for that.

Several teachers were within ear shot and heard every word the kids were saying. They did not react. No one cared about Landon, and if anything, they all treated him simply as a loner. Landon acted as if he did not care, but the look on his face often said otherwise.

"Did you hear that?" Anthony's color drained from his skin.

"Sounded like someone sat on a chip bag and popped it. What, are we back in junior high?" Eric asked while snorting with laughter.

Johnny shoved Eric and told him to shut up. The noise happened again. Suddenly, the cafeteria was silent.

The look on Anthony's face said it all. Utter fear ran through the cafeteria.

The pops began to move closer to the cafeteria. Everyone remained silent, frozen in fear. Peeking around the corner, a familiar face emerged. The boy not only had unwashed hair and puffy bags under his eyes, but gripped tightly in his pale, cold hands was a long rifle.

Landon.

As he emerged into the cafeteria, bullets began to erupt throughout the large, open room. The air was now filled with hysteria and chaos. What felt like a lifetime was ten minutes of sheer horror. As bodies laid near, a deep voice echoed the walls of the cafeteria.

"Police! If you can hear me, make yourself known." The police radio rattled with voices. "The shooter is down. I repeat, the shooter is down."

Students and teachers laid on the cold, tile floor. The once loud and vibrant cafeteria, filled with student chatter and laughter, was now filled with sorrow, winces, and shallow breathing.

The survivors were led to the parking lot. It was indistinguishable if tears were dripping from the faces of the fear-stricken students or if it was the rain. Students wandered the parking lot trying to find familiar, comforting faces—but some were never found . . . they were gone.

In the police briefing, it was discovered that before Landon reached his destination, the cafeteria, he entered classrooms where he shot out the window in the doors and unlocked the doors from the inside.

Two days later, as the rain trickled down, the caution tape had slowly fallen from the outside perimeter boundaries. Flowers and candles covered the sidewalk to remember those that were left in the school building. Although the windows had once created a beautiful aesthetic, they also created vulnerability which led to this tragic ending.

CHAPTER SUMMARY

A beautiful new school experiences the horror of a student with a gun expressing his internal rage. Some kids do not survive, and the aftermath reveals a community no longer in admiration of its new state of the art building.

QUESTIONS FOR REFLECTION

1. How can a planning committee and school leaders prioritize student safety with the design of a new school building?
2. What can school leaders do to equip a school building for optimal safety if it is not a new construction?
3. If you had been the school leader during this situation, how would you have handled the aftermath?
4. As a leader, how can we move forward to prevent situations like the one illustrated here from reoccurring?

REFERENCE

Kentucky Revised Statue 158.441 (2019) SB 1 School Safety and Resiliency Act. Kentucky Department of Education. Retrieved from https://education.ky.gov/school/sdfs/Pages/School-Safety-and-Resiliency-Act-(Senate-Bill,-2019).aspx.

Chapter 20

Anonymous Caller

J. P. Rader

School leaders have a cross to bear when following up on information that will potentially change the course of a faculty member or student's life.

What do you do when, on a Friday afternoon just as you are headed out to watch the high school soccer team play a home match, you are contacted from an anonymous caller accusing the head soccer coach of having an inappropriate relationship with an underage student in a previous school? That was the dilemma that faced Frank as he got the facts and tried to determine the next move to make. In his fifth year as the high school principal, Frank had never faced a child safety issue of this magnitude. As the phone call proceeded, it was clear that the implications of this accusation could be far-reaching.

The caller shared that "Coach Baxter was a young coach at our school in the late 1990s when he started spending a great deal of time with Tina, the sixteen-year-old striker on the soccer team. At first it was innocuous enough, as Coach Baxter had been a striker in college and it made sense that they would have some one-on-one sessions after practice, as well as private sessions other times during the season. Tina came from a difficult home life, so Coach Baxter provided an empathetic ear and shoulder to lean on, as well as providing the soccer feedback."

The caller continued. "It was only after one of the private sessions that feelings became more intense. Coach Baxter was only a few years older than Tina, but it was clear something was going on. I was one of Tina's teammates and saw how her life was left destitute after the men's soccer coach went to the school administration with discussion of the inappropriate relationship. The coach admitted to the relationship but claimed that nothing untoward had taken place."

"The administration put Coach Baxter on administrative leave for the rest of the year and then did not renew his contract. Tina was shattered by the accusations and rumors that flew around the school, and her life has never been the same since. I am calling you because I saw that Coach Baxter had been hired by your school and has been coaching several years. For the safety of the athletes, I beseech you to take action."

The caller hung up but not before revealing the name of the principal to contact who had handled the situation. The dilemma for Frank was complex. Coach Baxter had been at his school for six years, with a sterling record of behavior as a science teacher and coach, as well as multiple years at other schools. He was married, with three children, and had been a model citizen who added value to the school. Frank asked himself, "How valid is an accusation of this magnitude when it comes from an anonymous caller? Why did they wait so long to reach out? How vulnerable are all of us to attacks on our actions and, ultimately, our integrity, as leaders in the school?" These were troubling questions that Frank puzzled over as he walked out to the game.

The high school had in recent years implemented a comprehensive plan for child safety, composed of staff training and a short child safety course with video training, assessments, and role playing. A child safety team had been put together that met regularly, and posters with QR codes had been hung around the campus asking students and staff to pass along concerns and potential cases. A protocol had been put into place that would provide a step-by-step approach to dealing properly with child safety situations.

Most of the cases with which Frank had previously dealt involved parents who had threatened the safety of their children. This was different because it involved an active staff member. Frank knew his first steps were to call the previous school and verify the accuracy of the phone call. The facts of the case were verified, which led Frank to call in Coach Baxter for a difficult and painful conversation about the incident, now almost twenty years ago.

Coach Baxter admitted to the relationship but said to Frank that he had never crossed the line with Tina. Frank was left in a difficult situation—leave well enough alone and let the matter drop or seek counsel from his administrative team. He sought counsel from his team, which provided no definitive answers but did unfortunately lead to a leak of the information to his faculty and staff.

That evening Frank received multiple phone calls from irate teachers, staff, and finally parents demanding that Coach Baxter never be allowed contact with their children again and to be dismissed from his job. Frank was caught between a rock and a hard place. He had a good relationship with Coach Baxter, who had given good service to the school, but he also felt this could easily get out of hand. Coach Baxter, for his part, felt he was innocent and should remain on staff.

After consulting his child safety team, Frank decided to put Coach Baxter on temporary leave from his duties and to call in a neutral child safety team from a nearby school. By doing this, Frank created neutrality and fairness that was needed in this situation. This team came on campus and interviewed students who had been taught and coached by Coach Baxter. They also interviewed Tina and other members of the soccer team from the time of the ill-advised relationship.

Ultimately, the decision was made, after considering all of the evidence, that Coach Baxter's relationship with an underage player, even as far back as twenty years ago, had violated all of the child safety safeguards that had been put into place by the school. The school found a settlement for Coach Baxter's contract, put him on leave until the end of the year, did not renew his contract, and forbid him to be involved with students under the age of eighteen.

As Frank reflected on this sad ending to a popular coach's career, he realized that all actions as leaders in the school are scrutinized and held to a high standard, particularly in the current social media world in which information is so easily accessible. Ultimately, the role as administrators is to provide a safe environment for students to learn. If that gold standard is violated in any way, actions have to be taken.

Frank wondered how differently this situation would have resulted had he not felt compelled to revisit on the anonymous phone call. If something had happened again with Coach Baxter at his school because he ignored the call, how could he justify that? The administrator's cross is a difficult one to bear but must be shouldered for the sake of the students.

CHAPTER SUMMARY

A principal receives a phone call about a questionable teacher/student relationship at another school from twenty years ago. This teacher and coach, now at the principal's school, is a model citizen in the community. But a follow up investigation reveals the caller's revelations are accurate.

QUESTIONS FOR REFLECTION

1. Did Frank act responsibly as he assessed the situation he inherited?
2. Is it important to establish a child safety team and have protocols in place at your school? Does your school have such protocols?
3. Should there be a statute of limitations on actions that took place twenty years ago if the staff member in question has had a clean record since?

Chapter 21

It's Not Going to Happen Here

Bill Sullivan

> *There are horrific acts of violence occurring in schools throughout the United States. If the majority of teachers, administrators, and students in those locations were honest with themselves, they'd tell you that they did not believe that an active shooter incident would happen at their school. These individuals could be described as having experienced normalcy bias, and statistically speaking, they are correct in their assumption. Yet, when an active shooter does strike, the consequences can be devastating. And it is difficult, if not impossible, to accurately predict when and where these events will occur.*

It was just another school day with teachers and students going about their normal routines when an eighteen-year-old male crashed his truck into a ditch near their elementary school. The driver exited the truck with a semi-automatic rifle and a bag of ammunition and began shooting at two men who emerged from a nearby funeral home. The shooter had earlier texted his friend in Germany telling him that he had just shot his grandmother and was going to "shoot up" an elementary school. It was over an hour before he was shot and killed by law enforcement, and eighteen students and two teachers had been killed.

The ensuing review of this incident exposed numerous failures on the part of law enforcement, school officials, and school personnel (Texas House of Representatives Investigative Committee, 2022). However, this horrific event could have potentially been stopped, or at a minimum, the gunman's entry delayed, allowing additional time for law enforcement to respond and school personnel to announce and complete their lock down drill—properly securing their school. In this mass shooting incident, if the shooters entry into the school had been delayed an additional two to three minutes, law enforcement would have likely initiated contact with the shooter outside of the school.

This proactive approach could have eliminated or reduced the deaths of students and teachers. The only action required by school personnel was to follow the existing policy and ensure that the locks properly functioned and the classroom doors were secured. Prior to Nashville, Tennessee, no active shooter in the United States has breached a locked and secured door during the shooting rampage (Mallory, 2015; Martaindale, et al., 2017). Educators must ensure classroom doors are closed and locked from the beginning of class until the end of class. Routinely waiting to lock doors during lock down drills can have disastrous results.

TIMELINE

The following timeline and description of events is provided in an Associated Press article authored by Stengle and Bleiberg (2022).

- *Sometime after 11:00 a.m.:* The assailant shoots his grandmother in the face and police are called.
- *11:27 a.m.:* Video shows an unidentified female teacher propping open an exterior school door with a rock. This door would later be used by the shooter to enter the school.
- *11:28 a.m.:* One minute after the door is propped open, the shooter crashes his grandmother's truck into a nearby drainage ditch.
- *11:29 a.m.:* Two men exit the funeral home after hearing the crash. The shooter exits the vehicle and fires three rounds at the men but misses them. The unidentified teacher calls 911 and reports a man with a gun. After the woman determined the man had a gun, she reportedly removed the rock she had placed in the door. However, the door did not lock when it closed, and she apparently did not check to see if it was fully closed and secure.

Shortly after the crash, the elementary school coach (who was outdoors with a group of third graders) observed the shooter climb over the fence, raise his gun, and then begin shooting. The coach began running toward her classroom and reported what had occurred to the principal via radio. The principal unsuccessfully attempted to initiate lockdown, using the school's notification system. She then instructed the head custodian to ensure all doors were locked.

- *11:30 a.m.(approximately):* After school personnel learned about the man with a gun, primarily by word of mouth, teachers began lock down procedures. It is apparent that communication issues existed within the school, including problems with notification of the lockdown status and the presence of an active shooter.
- *11:32 a.m.:* The shooter fires multiple shots outside. Uvalde SWAT commander arrives and observes a man with a gun and retrieves his rifle and ammunition. The commander receives reports that the shooter is in, or near, the building, and he convenes with an Uvalde lieutenant and another officer.
- *11:33 a.m.:* The shooter enters the school through the exterior unlocked door that had previously been propped open with a rock. The shooter enters, exits, and reenters adjoining classrooms 111 and 112. The shooter spends approximately two and a half minutes and rapidly fires over 100 rounds. Room 111 was unlocked. However, one of the two teachers in Room 112, who died in the attack, reportedly had locked their door. Unfortunately, access to both classrooms was gained through the adjoining classroom 111. The male teacher in room 111, with the door unlocked, was shot but survived.
- *11:35 a.m.:* Two minutes after the shooter was reported to have gained entry into the school, three city police officers enter the school through the same west door used by the shooter. Prior to their entry, one of the officers reported hearing shots coming from within the school, and then a few muffled shots after entering the school.
- *11:36 a.m.:* Additional officers entered through the building's south door just three minutes after the shooter had entered the school. Four additional officers entered through the west door.
- *11:37 a.m.:* Officers from the west and south doors converge on the adjoining classrooms where the shooter is located, coming from both sides of the hallway toward Room 111 and Room 112. The shooter fires eleven rounds (apparently at officers), and two officers are grazed/struck with fragmentation from the shots. This results in the officers retreating down the hallway.
- *11:38 a.m.:* An unidentified officer states that the shooter is "contained in this office." Conversations are heard shortly after this stating, "We've got to get in there," and another officer responds that "DPS is sending their people." Ballistic shields and then a rifle and radio are requested by officers on scene. Concern is expressed because the shooter has a rifle, and the officers only have handguns.
- *11:40 a.m.:* The shooter fires one round; apparently, no attempt is made by officers in the hallway to enter Rooms 111 or 112.

- *11:43 a.m.:* Three additional officers enter the area from the east hallway. At this point it appears that there are police officers from at least four different agencies inside the school.

ASSESSMENT

Within four minutes of the shooter entering the building, law enforcement appeared to have the shooter contained to two rooms, 111 and 112. However, officers did not attempt to enter the rooms where the active shooter and victims were located. Within ten minutes of the shooter entering the school, it became apparent that communication issues existed. This included a lack of proper command and control, as well as the absence of an accurate assessment of the situation. These are crucial shortcomings in any critical incident response.

Police appear to have effectively contained the shooter, preventing him from gaining access to additional students and school personnel who are outside of Classrooms 111 and 112. However, by not gaining access to the classroom where the shooter is located and removing the threat, the injured individuals in the two classrooms cannot receive medical assistance, and any remaining survivors within the rooms are still subject to being shot and killed by the suspect or dying from existing wounds.

AN OUNCE OF PREVENTION IS WORTH A POUND OF CURE

While it is virtually impossible for schools to stop all armed intruder scenarios or acts of violence, simple actions can be taken to significantly reduce the number of individuals killed in mass shootings. Improvement can begin when teachers and school administrators eliminate the mindset of "it will not happen here." Improvement also involves refusing to accept existing critical shortcomings in security, and instead, ensuring that these shortcomings are addressed without delay.

This preventive approach includes the development of effective policies, security procedures/protocols, implementation of effective training (to both school personnel and all first responders associated with response efforts), and incorporation of effective security measures—including the use of layered physical security. The more layers that exist to deter and delay potential aggressors, particularly external threats, from gaining access to students and school personnel, the better the chance that responding officers will have the opportunity to stop an active shooter before they can gain access to the students and school personnel.

For example, the fence that the gunman scaled in the shooting created a slight delay in his attempt to access students. If, instead, the fence was substantial in height and incorporated the use of barbed wire or another means to deter and/or delay entry, it would have improved the chance of officers arriving on scene and initiating contact with the shooter before the aggressor gained access to the school. And, if all exterior doors had been properly locked, the shooter may have been unable to gain access into the school building.

Furthermore, had all the interior classrooms been locked and secured, it would have decreased the shooter's access to students and staff within the rooms, increased the delay, and/or eliminated the attempt to gain entry. Remember, at the time of this event, no active shooter in the United States has breached a locked and secured door during the shooting rampage (Final Report, Sandy Hook Advisory Commission, 2015; Martaindale, et.al., 2017). Educators must ensure their classroom doors are closed and locked from the beginning of class until the end of class, as well as exterior doors locked throughout the school day. Routinely waiting to lock doors until during lockdown drills can result in a disaster.

LESSONS LEARNED

Examining the scenario above and the timelines provided, it is highly probable that the number of deaths caused by the shooter would have been significantly reduced, or even eliminated, if the exterior and classroom doors were securely locked. It is impossible to make a school 100 percent safe or secure; however, a school can improve existing levels of security and significantly reduce the vulnerability and tragic consequences from school shooter incidents.

This safer culture can be accomplished by effectively utilizing layered security, improving command and control issues including communications, developing effective policies and procedures, and requiring the appropriate training of all personnel involved, including both school personnel and first responders.

Training should additionally incorporate the use of multiagency and multidisciplinary responses, and the utilization of progressive scenarios where the difficulty of situations and complexity of required tasks and responses increase as the participants' capabilities grow. This inclusion of progressive joint training will improve the overall efficiency and effectiveness of response activities by the various entities who are required to work together during a critical incident. Last, but not least, do not fall into the mindset of normalcy bias, thinking that "it will not happen here."

CHAPTER SUMMARY

A school is attacked by a shooter as he finds an exterior door and inside classroom door unlocked. By the time first responders sort out the details and stop the perpetrator, lives have been lost. Simple proactive measures would have prevented many, if not all, of the fatalities.

QUESTIONS FOR REFLECTION

1. Do you believe that your school is properly prepared for an active shooter incident?
2. What preventive actions can you personally take to improve your school's preparation for and response to active shooter incidents?
3. What preventive actions should your school's teachers and aides take to improve upon your school's preparation for and response to active shooter incidents?
4. What preventive actions should your school's administrators take to improve upon your school's preparation for and response to active shooter incidents?

REFERENCES

Malloy, G. D. P. (2015). Final report of the Sandy Hook advisory commission.
Martaindale, M. H., Sandel, W. L., & Blair, J. P. (2017). Active shooter events in the workplace: Findings and policy implications. *Journal of Business Continuity and Emergency Planning, 11*(1), 6–20.
Stengle, J., & Bleiberg, J. (2022, July 19). Timeline: Texas elementary school shooting, minute by minute. Retrieved from https://apnews.com/article/shootings-texas-education-school-6e37217b70e4977d985a1d1b50cc29fc
Texas House of Representatives. Interim Report. (2022). Investigative Committee on the Robb Elementary Shooting. Retrieved from https://house.texas.gov/_media/pdf/committees/reports/87interim/Robb-Elementary-Investigative-Committee-Report.pdf

Chapter 22

Cell Phone Safety

Myram Brady, Rachel Addison-Miller, and Pamela Puryear

> *Everyday habits seem so . . . so harmless. But they can be an ever-present danger.*

It was Mrs. Taylor's first year in the classroom as a high school teacher, and things were going well. She had a classroom rule to "be attentive," and students knew that this meant no cell phones were allowed during instructional time. However, today something was off. A group of girls were crowded around Tiffany in the back of the room, and she was crying. Mrs. Taylor went to investigate, but no one would say what was happening. She broke up the group and got everyone back on task. However, there was still a feeling in the room that something was wrong.

A few minutes later, another student approached Mrs. Taylor. She explained that when Tiffany went to the bathroom, she called her boyfriend. They got into a fight and her boyfriend, who was a few years older and out of high school, threatened her. He sent her text messages saying that he was coming to the school, and she was to sneak out and leave, and if she didn't, he had a knife and would kill her. Once Mrs. Taylor realized the severity of the situation, she immediately contacted administration in the building.

The entire school was quickly placed in lockdown and police were notified. Administration seized Tiffany's phone so that she could not contact her boyfriend. Mrs. Taylor quickly pulled her blinds and made sure that each window was locked. The building was all ground level, and her classroom windows faced the road with easy access. As students sheltered, Mrs. Taylor prepped them to fight in case the boyfriend somehow breached the room.

Time seemed to pass slowly, as tensions were high and students were frightened, but as sirens began to sound outside, there was a peace that could be felt. Local law enforcement stayed in the building while a hunt began for Tiffany's boyfriend. Police found him soon after, and he did have a knife on him. Thankfully, he did not try to enter the classroom and instead fled the scene. Tiffany's parents were notified of the incident and asked to come pick her up along with her cell phone. The boyfriend was banned from stepping foot on school property thereafter.

Tiffany and the boy parted ways and no further incidents occurred between them. Mrs. Taylor, however, continued to deal with cell phone issues in her classroom and school. Students began cyberbullying, creating drama and distractions. They would text each other and meet in the hallways to fight. Inappropriate photos of other students would be passed around through online apps. Even when Mrs. Taylor required cell phones to be placed in a holder at the front of the room, students found ways around it. Mrs. Taylor felt that the administration was not doing enough to assist with cell phone usage and issues.

RESEARCH AND RECOMMENDATIONS

Cell phones have great benefits, but as with everything, consequences are still present. These consequences can quickly outweigh the benefits. So, how can we as educators work to make cell phones a beneficial tool for a student's education? One way is to ensure that there are proper safeguards in place while also walking a tedious line.

A study conducted by Beland and Murphy (2016) showed that a phone ban does increase test scores by up to 14.23 percent for underachieving students, while those in the top quintile were not impacted. Banning cell phone usage does not negatively impact achievement. In fact, it helps to lower the achievement gap and does not negatively impact students' academics. However, a student's emotional well-being may be compromised with a cell phone ban. "Nomophobia" is the fear of not being able to use one's phone. This can cause behavioral issues, anxiety, and inappropriate use of cell phones (Carels, 2019). As technology is more ingrained into our lives, the more impact that nomophobia is likely to have.

A 2021 (Yadav et al.) study on the impact cell phones have on behavior and academic achievement showed a significant relationship between mobile phone dependency and behavioral changes and decreased academic achievement. Prepandemic, cell phones were not as commonplace in the classroom. During the pandemic, cell phones were unavoidable for students. Students used their cell phones to complete assignments, as well as keep up with their friends on social media, playing video games, listening to music, and watching videos.

In many classrooms across the country postpandemic, cell phones are used as instructional tools. Educational games like Quizlet, Kahoot, and EdPuzzle, just to name a few, enhance classroom learning and engagement. Unfortunately, students are now so dependent on their cell phones, breaking the habit of not using cell phones is incredibly difficult and can cause additional behavioral issues.

Most school districts have a written cellphone policy. In 2020, a study reported that "90% of principals in middle and high schools have restrictions on cellphone usage. Over 80% of these principals believe that cellphone usage during school has negative consequences on social development and academics" (Clayburn, 2022). Souvra Sengupta, an associate professor of psychiatry and pediatrics at the University of Buffalo stated, "Cellphones are a drug addiction in their hand. Kids have everything at their fingertips. A lot of social technology—whether its social media or streaming video games—they are all designed to provide a big dose of dopamine very quickly" (Clayburn, 2022).

Another especially egregious problem is cell phone cameras. There have been cases across the United States where students take videos of fights and pictures in private areas, such as locker rooms or bathrooms. Students will then share these videos and pictures with their friends electronically. This raises legal issues of privacy, sexual harassment, and theft of proprietary information (Obringer & Coffey, 2008).

Parents agree that cell phones should be allowed in schools. They allow parents to be able to get in contact with students whenever they deem it necessary. Ken Trump, president of the school safety consulting firm National School Safety and Security Services, says, "a student's focus should not be on their phone during a potential school emergency. Parents are not realizing that the use of a cell phone could make a child distracted and less safe in school. One hundred percent of their attention should be on the directions from adults" (Clayburn, 2022). On the other side of this debate, school shootings at Virginia Tech and Uvalde, Texas found that students were calling 911 to let law enforcement know about the shooter and where the shooter was located.

Some states have policies that impact the "after" procedures regarding cell phone issues. For example, if a student were to make threats via their cell phone into a group chat or to an individual student, there is a protocol that is followed. In Kentucky, immediate action is taken by the administration if a threat is reported to them. First, the student is brought to the office and the phone is confiscated. The administration then will contact the school system's director of pupil personnel and the school resource officer (SRO).

If something is found on the student's cellphone that is credible, like a threat, then the administration and the SRO will speak with the student. If the student is under the age of eighteen, the parents must give permission for the SRO to speak with that student. If the student is eighteen or over, the parent does not need to be contacted for permission, but in almost every case the parent is called anyway. If the police deem that a threat is credible, charges can be brought against the student. The school will place the student on a ten-day suspension and will conduct a hearing before the school board for expulsion. If the board finds that the threat is not credible, the student must complete a risk assessment before returning to school.

Overall, cell phones pose a safety risk for the school. There are some potential benefits of cell phones providing educational enhancements and allowing students access to the police, but studies show that there are far more negatives that outweigh these positives. It is important to note that while cell phones pose a safety risk, outlawing them in schools may also present a public relations nightmare with parents and the community. All schools should regularly reevaluate their cell phone policy as technology changes over the years and consider recent research on safety and student achievement.

CHAPTER SUMMARY

An example of student harassment and threatening via cell phone communication is shared, followed by recommendations from research on how schools can prevent overuse of cell phones in the school setting.

QUESTIONS FOR REFLECTION

1. Does your state have guidance or policies for administration regarding threats via cell phones?
2. What is the current cell phone policy in your school?
3. Have you witnessed cell phone safety issues firsthand?
4. Would the current policy in your school have prevented this safety issue if enforced?
5. When was your cell phone policy implemented or updated last?
6. What recommendations would you make to combat cell phone safety issues in your school?

REFERENCES

Beland, L. P., & Murphy, R. (2016). Ill communication: Technology, distraction, & student performance. *Labour Economics, 41*, 61–76.

Carels, B. (2019). Changing our mindset in regards to cellphones in the classroom. *BU Journal of Graduate Studies in Education, 11*(2), 9–12.

Clayburn, C. (2022, October 20). *Cellphones in School: What to Know*. US News. https://www.usnews.com/education/best-high-schools/articles/cellphones-in-school-what-to-know

Obringer, S. J., & Coffey, K. M. (2007). Cell Phones in American High Schools: A National Survey. *The Journal of Technology Studies, 33*, 41–47.

Smale, W. T., Hutcheson, R., & Russo, C. J. (2021). Cell phones, student rights, and school safety: Finding the right balance. *Canadian Journal of Educational Administration and Policy*, 195, 49–64.

Yadav, M. S., Kodi, S. M., & Deol, R. (2021). Impact of mobile phone dependence on behavior and academic performance of adolescents in selected schools of Uttarakhand, India. *Journal of Education and Health Promotion, 10*, 327. https://doi.org/10.4103/jehp.jehp_915_20

Chapter 23

Security Scare Internet Style

Holly Hunt and Kim Puckett

> *Because children with disabilities may be more prone to loneliness (Margalit & Al-Yagon, 2002), they may be especially vulnerable to the harmful advances of online users who show a seemingly benign interest in their lives.*

Situated on a college campus, Southside is a school unlike any other in the state. The history of the school, and its actual building, dates back to 1906. As a training facility for the university, students have access to the school as part of their college course work. The building has many entrances, and for safety purposes, each of those doors are equipped with numbered keypads so that students, faculty, and staff can enter the building. Keypad codes, which are only active during the school day, are set periodically by the district safety team, and students, faculty, and staff are provided the code at the beginning of each semester.

Southside is a "one-to-one" device school. All students receive a MacBook Air at registration and are provided with a school email address. Southside students are also required to sign an electronic user agreement upon receiving their school device. This agreement states that the device, as well as the email account, will be used solely for school purposes.

Conner Gibson is a thirteen-year-old male student receiving special education services under the diagnosis of a mild mental disability. His parents have chosen an alternate track diploma, and he is completely immersed in the traditional classroom setting for most of the day. This allows him to interact with students of all abilities and backgrounds. While students are aware of Conner's disability, they fully accept him in their classrooms and protect him from bullying or dangerous behavior.

Recently, school administrators were made aware of a potentially dangerous situation regarding Conner. Classmates informed the school counselor, Mrs. Thompson, that Conner had been emailing a YouTube influencer, and they were concerned that he was sharing personal information that might jeopardize his safety. Upon further investigation, administrators discovered that he had indeed emailed the influencer not only his home address, but the address of the school as well, and also the code to the door keypads.

Administrators requested that Mr. Brown, the director of technology, review Conner's email history to determine if similar emails were sent to anyone else. The influencer had not responded, nor had there been any previous correspondence. Nonetheless, administrators knew that this could potentially lead to a significant safety issue for both Conner and the school.

Upon discovering the emails, administrators immediately contacted Ms. Tyler, the district safety coordinator, and requested that a new code be created for the many keypads throughout the building. Conner's special education teacher, Mrs. Exum, and Mrs. Thompson, the school counselor, spoke to him about the incident. While Conner did admit to emailing the influencer, neither Mrs. Exum nor Mrs. Thompson believed he realized the seriousness of his actions. After communicating with his parents, Mr. and Mrs. Gibson, the team agreed to reconvene with the school principal the following day.

The next day, Dr. Grayson, the school principal, contacted Conner's mother to discuss the situation. Dr. Grayson shared her concerns with the parent about Conner's lack of understanding the dangers of this situation. Both agreed that it was impossible for Conner to understand the seriousness of his actions without a consequence. Conner's mom, Dr. Grayson, and Mrs. Exum agreed that it was important for Conner's future, not only at Southside, but as an adult, for him to understand that his actions could put himself and others in danger.

Mrs. Gibson felt that if Conner could verbally communicate why his actions were wrong, as well as explain the school and technology rules, she would feel more confident that this action would not be repeated. She also felt it was necessary to emphasize this behavior at home and take precautions with his personal devices.

Mr. and Mrs. Gibson, as well as Dr. Grayson, agreed that assigning Conner a Saturday school detention with Mrs. Exum would allow him to better understand the seriousness of his behaviors. As the school principal and special education teacher, Dr. Grayson and Mrs. Exum designed a plan of action regarding what this detention would encompass, focusing specifically on safe use of technology and potential situations that could arise from sharing personal information with strangers.

CHAPTER SUMMARY

Southside school, located on a college campus, finds itself in a scary situation when a special education student emails the school address and door codes to a YouTube influencer. Due to concerned fellow students, administrators, teachers, the safety coordinator, technology support personnel and the parents, this team was able to maintain school safely while educating the student on safe usage of technology.

QUESTIONS FOR REFLECTION

1. Does your school have safety trainings specifically for students with special needs?
2. How do you ensure that this student population understands the importance and severity of these safety precautions?
3. How would you have handled this situation differently?
4. What disciplinary actions would you have implemented and why?
5. Does your school provide training for students and staff in the domain of online "best practice"?

Chapter 24

Student Voice

Toni Konz Tatman

In a school setting, the best laid plans often take a back seat to current events. A fight. A weapon found in a backpack. A school shooting . . . The debate begins: How can we increase school safety? An important voice is frequently missing in that conversation.

—Toni Konz Tatman

The agenda for the May 31, 2022, meeting of the Kentucky Department of Education (KDE) Commissioner's Student Advisory Council had been set weeks in advance. There would be a discussion on further amplifying student voice—an end of the year reflection, followed by a conversation among students and education officials about co-designing an ideal learning space. And then the school shooting in Uvalde, Texas happened a week prior.

"We use this group a lot, advising us on how we can make better policy decisions for KDE," Commissioner Jason E. Glass said to the group of two dozen high school students gathered at the agency's office in Frankfort, Kentucky. Dr. Glass added, "There is one change to the agenda . . . toward the end, we have the item, 'co-designing an ideal school or learning space.' It is something we are going to hold on. Instead . . . I really want to have some time for you to dialogue [on what happened in Texas]."

The group, made up of sophomores, juniors, and seniors from each of the seven Kentucky Supreme Court districts, meets monthly to advise the commissioner of education on issues relevant to high school students. Throughout the year, most meetings are held virtually through Microsoft Teams and livestreamed as a public meeting on the KDE Media Portal. Previous council reports and recommendations have focused on issues related to mental health and efforts to strengthen diversity, equity, inclusion, and belonging in

Kentucky public schools. However, the May 31, 2022, meeting was in-person, and it was the last one of the 2021–2022 academic year.

"I would like for this group to have a conversation [about the Uvalde shooting] and perhaps organize your time into a white paper or a position paper that makes recommendations to policy makers, from a student perspective, of how we can better secure our schools and make them safer spaces. What are some steps we can take?" Glass said.

He added, "In spite of all the good intentions and energy and research that adults are doing on this issue, you are the ones who are spending the most time in school right now, and you are the best experts around student experiences and how it could be made more secure."

The commissioner's comments on the school shooting was followed by a mindful moment activity conducted by Damien Sweeney, Ed.D., a former high school counselor and program coordinator for Comprehensive School Counseling at KDE. In his current role as director of diversity, equity, inclusion, and belonging at the agency, Sweeney often does check-ins with the student advisory council.

"We need proximity. We need to be able to process what's happened, talk about it, and know we're not alone in those feelings," Sweeney said.

Students shared a range of reactions—from anger to sadness to disgust to outrage to disbelief to helplessness to exhaustion (Kentucky Department of Education, Commissioner's Student Advisory Council Summary Minutes, and Grider-Jones).

"I think it's really scary as a student that we practice all of these drills, that we practice red codes and lockdowns for the possibility of this becoming a reality, and it's still happening, despite our efforts to be safe in school," said a 2022 graduate from a rural Kentucky high school.

Another recent graduate of a Kentucky school said that having these conversations with students, although hard emotionally, is important and should be encouraged by schools.

"We are the ones being affected the most," she said.

By the end of the meeting, three categories were created to focus on those topics of most interest: Proactive events before a school shooting, actions in the event of an active shooter, and recovery from the effects of a school shooting. Students committed to diving deeper into those topics over the summer and fall then began to write a collective policy recommendation for legislators and other education stakeholders to read.

At the group's next meeting in August, they heard from Christina Weeter, the director of the Division of Student Success in the Office of Continuous Improvement and Support at KDE. She discussed the background, purpose, and current school safety measures outlined in Kentucky's School Safety and Resiliency Act (SSRA). She noted how multiple stakeholders and agencies outlined in the SSRA, passed by the Kentucky General Assembly in 2019, work to strengthen school campuses by promoting both physical safety and students' psychological well-being.

In particular, Weeter discussed how KDE's trauma-informed toolkit, required as part of SSRA, offers school districts guidance, strategies, and training on trauma-informed practices regarding (among others) discipline policies, active shooter trainings, and how to ensure students who may have been exposed to trauma are provided appropriate supports at school (Kentucky Department of Education, 2022).

The students then discussed the current draft of their collective school safety policy recommendations with Commissioner Glass, Deputy Commissioner Dr. Thomas Woods-Tucker, and other KDE officials who worked with the students on this project, including Dr. Meredith Brewer (director of policy), Brian Perry (director of government affairs), and several members of the agency's Division of Communications team.

During the next two meetings, students participated in group breakout sessions with KDE staff, who also answered student questions and offered suggestions on additional resources. Suggestions were also shared on how to disseminate the final document, including how to share it with school and district leaders and how to lead targeted presentations to key constituents who may have the authority to implement the students' recommendations.

At their January 24, 2023 meeting in Frankfort, the Commissioner's Student Advisory Council presented its report on potential actions to increase school safety. In the audience was State Representative James Tipton, chairman of the Kentucky House Education Committee.

The report followed a year where schools across the nation experienced 170 incidents of gunfire on school grounds, according to Everytown Research and Policy. Those incidents resulted in 55 deaths and 145 injuries (Everytown for Gun Safety Support Fund, 2023).

Council member Peter Jefferson, a sophomore at Henry Clay High School (Fayette County), said he and his fellow council members wanted to make an impact on what is a growing problem in schools.

"Something is happening," Jefferson said of violent incidents in schools. "How can we make sure that it doesn't happen to us and minimize the effects of it, if it does?"

"We all had a lot of big emotions and we needed somewhere to put that," said council member Malley Taylor, a junior at Craft Academy (Rowan County). "We realized we needed to use our voices for change."

The students presented three different categories of recommendations: before an incident, during an incident, and after an incident. Before an incident occurs, the group said there should be better promotion of the state's STOP Tipline and an improvement in the rate of intervention in concerning behaviors. They also recommended supporting gun control (Breunig et al., n.d.). For during an incident, the group suggested an improvement on active shooter drills, as well as better training for first responders. In addition, the students recommended that officials establish a clear notification system for students and parents.

Citing research from the *Journal of Adolescent Health*, council members said the majority of active shooter drills are ineffective and sometimes do more harm than good. Council members also said the majority of students felt they did not understand the benefits of active shooter drills and felt emotional distress because of them. The students recommended drills that offer a more realistic simulation of an active shooter situation.

After an incident, the student group offered three recommendations: Provide mental health support, host town hall meetings, and repair and rebuild the school building.

"Our main goal is to make sure that everyone is getting a quality education," said council member Joud Dahleh, a senior at Ignite Academy (Boone County). "And you cannot have a quality education if you do not feel safe in your school building."

Commissioner Glass said including student voice when it comes to school safety is vital, as "they are the ones that are under the threat of this on a regular basis."

"We're proud of the work that they've done," he said. "I think they've shown how capable Kentucky students are at pulling together policy recommendations that are smart, well-vetted, and well-researched."

CHAPTER SUMMARY

In the midst of yet another school shooting in Uvalde, Texas, a group of about two dozen high school students from Kentucky are spurred into action. Over the course of seven months, the students conducted research independently and held discussions in breakout groups to develop a list of potential policy changes focused on three different categories of recommendations: Before an incident, during an incident, and after an incident. Those recommendations were laid out in a white paper, A Focus On School Safety, and presented to lawmakers and other policy makers.

QUESTIONS FOR REFLECTION

1. Can you think of a time when, as an educator, you included student voice as part of a discussion about school safety?

2. If you had been in Commissioner Glass' shoes on May 31, 2022, would you have chosen to amend the meeting's agenda in order to directly discuss the Uvalde school shooting with students? Why or why not?

REFERENCE

Breunig, Gavin, et al. (n.d.). "A Focus on School Safety." *Kentucky Department of Education*, https://education.ky.gov/CommOfEd/adv/Documents/Commissioner%27s%20Student%20Council/A%20Focus%20on%20School%20Safety.pdf. Accessed April 19, 2023.

Everytown for Gun Safety Support Fund. "The Impact of Gun Violence on Children and Teens." *Everytown Research & Policy*, May 29, 2019, https://everytownresearch.org/report/the-impact-of-gun-violence-on-children-and-teens/. Accessed April 19, 2023.

Kentucky Department of Education. "School Safety and Resiliency Act—Kentucky Department of Education." *Kentucky Department of Education*, August 2, 2022, https://education.ky.gov/school/sdfs/Pages/School-Safety-and-Resiliency-Act-(Senate-Bill,-2019).aspx. Accessed April 19, 2023.

Kentucky Department of Education Commissioner's Student Advisory Council presents recommendations to increase school safety. (2023). *Kentucky Teacher.* (2023, February 3). Retrieved April 23, 2023, from https://www.kentuckyteacher.org/news/2023/01/kdes-commissioners-student-advisory-council-presents-recommendations-to-increase-school-safety/

Lamb, A. (2022). "Kentucky students discuss school safety policy suggestions, relief efforts for flood-impacted districts." Edited by Toni Konz Tatman and Jennifer Ginn. *Kentucky Teacher*, August 23, 2022, https://www.kentuckyteacher.org/news/2022/08/kentucky-students-discuss-school-safety-policy-suggestions-relief-efforts-for-flood-impacted-districts/. Accessed 19 April 2023.

Lamb, A., & Caleb B. (2022). "KDE's Student Advisory Council discusses eastern Kentucky flood recovery, charter schools, school safety." Edited by Toni Konz Tatman. *Kentucky Teacher*, October 13, 2022, https://www.kentuckyteacher.org/news/2022/10/kdes-student-advisory-council-discusses-eastern-kentucky-flood-recovery-charter-schools-school-safety/. Accessed April 19, 2023.

Ragusa, J. (2023). "KDE's Commissioner's Student Advisory Council presents recommendations to increase school safety." Edited by Toni Konz Tatman and Jennifer Ginn. *Kentucky Teacher*, January 24, 2023, https://www.kentuckyteacher.org/news/2023/01/kdes-commissioners-student-advisory-council-presents-recommendations-to-increase-school-safety/. Accessed April 19, 2023.

Closing Thoughts

Sometimes, "the road less traveled" is not what we had imagined when we were in college and soon deciding on a career. Perhaps we dreamed of being a teacher—the perfect job (or so it had seemed when we were in elementary school as a student).

And then one day we found ourselves in front of a classroom. All of those teacher prep courses, required texts to digest, hours logged observing in schools, student teaching, learning how to develop the perfect lesson plan . . . No longer were they on our daily calendar of "things to do." That day, it was the real deal. That day, we "faced the music" and began to grow into our calling. We began the fulfilling, yet also demanding and stressful life of a talent scout, mentor, coach, role model, and parent figure—all rolled into one. But first and foremost, we were to be a gatekeeper, a fierce maintainer of safe space and culture for every student in our care.

And we can still do it, and do it well—if our classroom and school is a "hiding place," an incubator, a learning center far from the toxicity of brokenness—a place our students can call home.

The authors who have taken the time to share their experiences and expertise with us here have shown us how to pave a way for schools to be safer havens again. May we embrace the challenge.

APPENDICES

Promising Practices from the Kentucky Center for School Safety Bomb Threat Guidance: https://www.cisa.gov/sites/default/files/publications/dhs-doj-bomb-threat-guidance-brochure-2016-508.pdf

Elementary School Lockdown Workbook: https://kycss.org/ns/wp-content/uploads/2020/11/EMP-KCSS-Lockdowns-and-Elementary-Schools-Workbook.pdf

Human Trafficking: https://phoenixdreamcenter.org/human-trafficking/

Lockdown Basics: https://kycss.org/ns/wp-content/uploads/2022/07/EMP-Lockdown-Basic-Discussion-Principles-revised-5.5.2020.docx

Risk Assessment for Schools: https://kycss.org/ns/wp-content/uploads/2022/09/TRC-2022-2023-Risk-Assessment-7-6-22-Word.docx

Works Cited

Advisory Groups—Kentucky Department of Education. (n.d.). Retrieved April 23, 2023, from https://education.ky.gov/CommOfEd/adv/Pages/default.aspx

Akers, J. (2023). Kentucky Center for School Safety. Richmond.

Armstrong, T. (2019). School safety starts from within. *Educational Leadership*, 77(2), 48–52.

ASCD. (n.d.). *The whole child approach to education*. Retrieved April 23, 2023, from https://www.ascd.org/whole-child

Assistant Secretary for Public Affairs (ASPA). (2021, September 9). *Facts about bullying*. StopBullying.gov. Retrieved April 23, 2023, from https://www.stopbullying.gov/resources/facts#_Fast_Facts

Beland, L. P., & Murphy, R. (2016). Ill communication: Technology, distraction, & student performance. *Labour Economics*, 41, 61–76.

Bolman, L., & Deal, T. (2017). *Reframing organizations* (6th ed.). Josey-Bass.

Borum, R., Cornell, D. G., Modzeleski, W., & Jimerson, S. R. (2010). What can be done about school shootings?: A review of the evidence. *Educational Researcher*, 39(1), 27–37, https://doi.org/10.3102/0013189X09357620

Bradshaw, C. P., Debnam, K. J., Kush, J. M., & Johnson, S. L. (2022). Planning for a crisis, but preparing for every day: What predicts schools' preparedness to respond to a school safety crisis? *Frontiers in Communication*, 7, 1–5, https://doi.org/10.3389/fcomm.2022.765336

Brady, K. P., Ingle, W. K., & Pijanowski, J. (2021). Searches in public schools: Contemporary legal considerations for educators. In L. Stedrak, & J. Mezzina (Eds.), *Legal literacy for public school teachers*. Education Law Association.

Brenan, M. (2022, December 6). *Parent, student school safety concerns elevated*. Gallup.com. Retrieved April 23, 2023, from https://news.gallup.com/poll/399680/parent-studentschoolsafety-concerns-elevated.aspx

Breunig, Gavin, et al. (n.d.). "A Focus on School Safety." *Kentucky Department of Education*, https://education.ky.gov/CommOfEd/adv/Documents/Commissioner%27s%20Student%20Council/A%20Focus%20on%20School%20Safety.pdf. Accessed 19 April 2023.

Works Cited

Carels, B. (2019). Changing our mindset in regards to cellphones in the classroom. *BU Journal of Graduate Studies in Education, 11*(2), 9–12.

Clayburn, C. (2022, October 20). *Cellphones in School: What to Know.* US News. https://www.usnews.com/education/best-high-schools/articles/cellphones-in-school-what-to-know

Colwell, W. B., Brady, K. P., & Ingle, W. K. (2017). Searches in public schools. In J. Decker, M. Lewis, E. Shaver, A. Blankenship, & M. Paige (Eds.), *The principal's legal handbook* (6th ed.). Education Law Association.

Ellis, M. W., & Foster, D. (2023). School buildings, teachers, and asbestos exposure. Retrieved March 8, 2023, from https://mesothelioma.net/school-buildings-teachers-asbestos-exposure/

Everytown for Gun Safety Support Fund. "The Impact of Gun Violence on Children and Teens." *Everytown Research & Policy*, May 29, 2019, https://everytownresearch.org/report/the-impact-of-gun-violence-on-children-and-teens/. Accessed April 19, 2023.

Gessford J. B., Perry, G. H., & Knight, J. J. (2017). Child abuse. In J. Decker, M. Lewis, E. Shaver, A. Blankenship, & M. Paige (Eds.), *The principal's legal handbook* (6th ed.). Education Law Association.

Kentucky Department of Education, Commissioner's Student Advisory Council Summary Minutes, and GlyptusAnn Grider-Jones. "KENTUCKY DEPARTMENT OF EDUCATION." *Kentucky Department of Education*, 31 May 2022, https://education.ky.gov/CommOfEd/adv/Documents/Commissioner%27s%20Student%20Council/2022May31%20Commissioner%27s%20Student%20Advisory%20Council%20Summary.pdf. Accessed 18 April 2023.

Kentucky Department of Education. "School Safety and Resiliency Act - Kentucky Department of Education." *Kentucky Department of Education*, 2 August 2022, https://education.ky.gov/school/sdfs/Pages/School-Safety-and-Resiliency-Act-(Senate-Bill,-2019).aspx. Accessed 19 April 2023.

Kentucky Department of Education (KDE). (2023-a). *Kentucky facilities inventory and classification system.*

Kentucky Department of Education (KDE). (2023-b). *Updated unofficial state report.* Retrieved on February 8, 2023 from https://education.ky.gov/districts/fac/Pages/Kentucky%20Facilities%20Inventory%20and%20Classification%20System.aspx

Kentucky Department of Education Commissioner's Student Advisory Council presents recommendations to increase school safety. (2023). *Kentucky Teacher.* (2023, February 3). Retrieved April 23, 2023, from https://www.kentuckyteacher.org/news/2023/01/kdes-commissioners-student-advisory-council-presents-recommendations-to-increase-school-safety/

Kentucky Revised Statue 158.441. (2019). SB 1 School Safety and Resiliency Act. Kentucky Department of Education. (n.d.). Retrieved from https://education.ky.gov/school/sdfs/Pages/School-Safety-and-Resiliency-Act-%28Senate-Bill%2019%29.aspx#:~:text=In%202019%2C%20the%20Kentucky%20General%20Assembly%20passed%20the,many%20agencies%20that%20work%20with%20districts%20and%20schools

Kentucky Student Voice Team. (2021). *Coping with COVID-19 student-to-student study*. 2nd ed. Retrieved April 23, 2023, from https://globaluploads.webflow.com/630e58db6406d5a8f8a3ab90/6323b53b768816703e06a9ed_Coping%20With%20COVID-19%20Executive%20Summary.pdf

Kutsyuruba, B., Klinger, D. A., & Hussain, A. (2015). Relationships among school climate, school safety, and student achievement and well☐being: a review of the literature. *Review of Education, 3*(2), 103–35

KYSafe. (2022). *Consultative*. Retrieved March 10, 2023 from https://kysafe.ky.gov/services/Pages/consult.aspx

Lai, Esnard, A.-M., Wyczalkowski, C., Savage, R., & Shah, H. (2019). Trajectories of school recovery after a natural disaster: Risk and protective factors: School recovery after a natural disaster. *Risk, Hazards & Crisis in Public Policy, 10*(1), 32–51. https://doi.org/10.1002/rhc3.12158

Lamb, A. (2022). "Kentucky students discuss school safety policy suggestions, relief efforts for flood-impacted districts." Edited by Toni Konz Tatman and Jennifer Ginn. *Kentucky Teacher*, August 23, 2022, https://www.kentuckyteacher.org/news/2022/08/kentucky-students-discuss-school-safety-policy-suggestions-relief-efforts-for-flood-impacted-districts/. Accessed 19 April 2023.

Lamb, A., & Caleb B. (2022). "KDE's Student Advisory Council discusses eastern Kentucky flood recovery, charter schools, school safety." Edited by Toni Konz Tatman. *Kentucky Teacher*, October 13, 2022, https://www.kentuckyteacher.org/news/2022/10/kdes-student-advisory-council-discusses-eastern-kentucky-flood-recovery-charter-schools-school-safety/. Accessed April 19, 2023.

Madfis, E. (2016). "It's better to overreact": School officials' fear and perceived risk of rampage attacks and the criminalization of American public schools. *Critical Criminology 24*, 39–55. https://doi.org/10.1007/s10612-015-9297-0

Malloy, G. D. P. (2015). Final report of the Sandy Hook advisory commission.

Maor, M. (2012). Policy overreaction. *Journal of Public Policy, 32*(3), 231–59.

Martaindale, M. H., Sandel, W. L., & Blair, J. P. (2017). Active shooter events in the workplace: Findings and policy implications. *Journal of Business Continuity and Emergency Planning, 11*(1), 6–20.

Maslow, A. H. (1943). A theory of human motivation. *Psychological Review, 50*(4), 370–96. doi: 10.1037/h0054346

McInerney, M., & McKlindon, A. (n.d.). Unlocking the door to learning: Trauma-informed classrooms & transformation schools. *Education Law Center.* https://www.elc-pa.org/resource/unlocking-the-door-to-learning-trauma-informed-classrooms-and-transformational-schools/

Meier, K. J., O'Toole, Jr, L. J., & Hicklin, A. (2010). *I've seen fire and I've seen rain: Public management and performance after a natural disaster.* https://doi.org/10.1177/0095399709349027

Mirsky, L. (2011). Building safer, saner schools. *Educational Leadership, 69*(1), 45–49.

Missouri Department of Labor. (2021). *What is an imminent danger condition, a serious or other-than-serious hazard?* Retrieved March 10, 2023 from https:

//laboranswers.mo.gov/hc/en-us/articles/4405252992535-What-is-an-imminent-danger-condition-a-serious-or-other-than-serious-hazard-

Moritz-Rabson, D., & Phifer, D. (February 15, 2019). Who is Gary Martin? Aurora shooting suspect identified by police. *Newsweek.* Retrieved April 2023 https://web.archive.org/web/20190217062007/https://www.newsweek.com/who-aurora-mass-shooter-1333550

National Association of State Directors of Teacher Education and Certification. (2015). Model Code of Ethics for Educators (1st Ed.). Retrieved January 4, 2023 http://www.nasdtec.net/?page=MCEE_Doc#PrinI

The National Child Traumatic Stress Network. (n.d.). *Tornado Resources.* Retrieved January 10, 2023, from https://www.nctsn.org/what-is-child-trauma/trauma-types/disasters/tornado-resources

National Policy Board for Educational Administration. (2015). Professional Standards for Educational Leaders 2015. Author.

National Scientific Council on the Developing Child. (2005/2004). *Excessive stress disrupts the architecture of the developing brain: Working paper 3.* Updated Edition. http://www.developingchild.harvard.edu

Obringer, S. J., & Coffey, K. M. (2007). Cell Phones in American High Schools: A National Survey. *The Journal of Technology Studies, 33,* 41–47.

Olweus, D. (2013). School Bullying: Development and Some Important Challenges. *Annual Review of Clinical Psychology, 9*(1), 751–80

Ragusa, J. (2023). "KDE's Commissioner's Student Advisory Council presents recommendations to increase school safety." Edited by Toni Konz Tatman and Jennifer Ginn. *Kentucky Teacher*, January 24, 2023, https://www.kentuckyteacher.org/news/2023/01/kdes-commissioners-student-advisory-council-presents-recommendations-to-increase-school-safety/. Accessed April 19, 2023.

Research. (S)HE Matters. (n.d.). Retrieved April 23, 2023, from https://shemattersky.org/research

Rivera, B. (2011). *Teacher perceptions of the American School Counselor Association's national model in an urban setting* [published master's theses]. SUNY Brockport.

School safety starts from within. ASCD. (n.d.). Retrieved April 23, 2023, from http://www.ascd.org/el/articles/school-safety-starts-from-within

Smale, W. T., Hutcheson, R., & Russo, C. J. (2021). Cell phones, student rights, and school safety: Finding the right balance. *Canadian Journal of Educational Administration and Policy,* 195, 49–64.

Stengle, J., & Bleiberg, J. (2022, July19). Timeline: Texas elementary school shooting, minute by minute. Retrieved from https://apnews.com/article/shootings-texas-education-school-6e37217b70e4977d985a1d1b50cc29fc

Texas House of Representatives. Interim Report. (2022). Investigative Committee on the Robb Elementary Shooting. Retrieved from https://house.texas.gov/_media/pdf/committees/reports/87interim/Robb-Elementary-Investigative-Committee-Report.pdf

The National Child Traumatic Stress Network. (n.d.). *Tornado Resources.* Retrieved January 10, 2023, from https://www.nctsn.org/what-is-child-trauma/trauma-types/disasters/tornado-resources

United States Department of Labor. (n.d.). *Occupational Safety and Health Administrations: About OSHA.* Retrieved March 10, 2023, from https://www.osha.gov/about osha

Wink, M. N., LaRusso, M. D., & Smith, R. L. (2021). Teacher empathy and students with problem behaviors: Examining teachers' perceptions, responses, relationships, and burnout. *Psychology in the Schools, 58*(8), 1575–96.

Yadav, M. S., Kodi, S. M., & Deol, R. (2021). Impact of mobile phone dependence on behavior and academic performance of adolescents in selected schools of Uttarakhand, India. *Journal of Education and Health Promotion, 10,* 327. https://doi.org/10.4103/jehp.jehp_915_20

AUTHOR BIOGRAPHIES

Addison-Miller, Rachel (MBA, Morehead State University). Business instructor, Lee County High School (Ky.). Pursuing doctorate in educational leadership with MSU.

Ballinger, Carrie (Ed.D, Murray State University). Superintendent of Rockcastle County Schools (Ky.). Former Elementary Director, Model Lab School, Eastern Kentucky University.

Brady, Myram (Ed.S, Asbury University). Principal, Lawrence County High School (Ky.). Pursuing doctorate in educational leadership at Morehead State University.

Burns, Ann (Ed.D, Eastern Kentucky University). Associate professor and leadership programs coordinator at Eastern Kentucky University.

Burton, Brett (Ed.D, Northern Illinois University). Assistant professor and program director for educational administration at Xavier University.

Conway-Cunningham, Krystal (MA, Morehead State University, Kentucky State University). Teaches high school math/science, pursuing her doctorate in school administration from MSU.

Darnall, Byron (Ed.D, Seton Hall University). Associate commissioner, office of educator licensure and effectiveness. Former principal, Franklin-Simpson High School (Ky.).

Drury, Christina (Ed.S, University of the Cumberlands). Principal, Westridge Elementary in Franklin County (Ky.).

Hamilton, Charles "Chuck" (Ed.D, University of Kentucky). Associate professor, graduate studies, Campbellsville University. CU's Faculty of the Year, 2018.

Howell, Rebecca Martin (Ed.S, Morehead State University). Principal, Oakview Elementary, Ashland Independent (Ky.).

Hub, Kevin (Ed.D, Spaulding University). Executive-in-residence, associate professor educational leadership, Eastern Kentucky University. Graduate of West Point Academy.

Hunt, Holli (Ed.D, University of the Cumberlands). Secondary principal, Model Laboratory School at Eastern Kentucky University.

Ingle, William Kyle (PhD, Florida State University). Professor of P–12 educational leadership at the University of Louisville.

Kessinger, Michael W. (Ed.D, University of Kentucky). Associate professor of educational leadership, Morehead State University, and coordinator of MSU's educational leadership program.

Lauck, Taylor (Ed.S, Morehead State University). District instructional coach, Franklin County Schools (Ky.), and a doctoral student at Morehead State University.

Morris, Abigail (Ed.D, Murray State University). Assistant professor at Murray State University, College of Education and Health Science.

Puckett, Kim (Ph.D, Ecole Superieure Robert de Sorbon). Assistant superintendent, Model Lab School, Eastern Kentucky University, and an adjunct professor in special education for EKU.

Puryear, Pamela (Rank I, Eastern Kentucky University). Math teacher, Lawrence County High School (Ky.). Pursuing her doctorate in educational leadership at Morehead State University.

Rader, James Paul (Ed.D, Morehead State University). Head of school at International Community School (Singapore), in the Network of International Christian Schools (NICS).

Stewart, Veda (Ed.D, Eastern Kentucky University). Director for educator recruitment and development for the Kentucky Department of Education.

Sullivan, Bill (Ed.D, Eastern Kentucky University). Associate professor, Eastern Kentucky University, Homeland Security Program. Served with Kentucky state police for twenty-five years.

Sullivan, Stephanie (Ed.D, Murray State University). Assistant professor, MSU Education Administration program. Chair of Department of Early Childhood and Elementary.

Tatman, Toni Konz (BA, University of Southern Mississippi). Chief communications officer, Kentucky Department of Education. Oversees the Commissioner's Student Advisory Council.

Thomas, Franklin B. (Ed.D, Eastern Kentucky University). Assistant professor, School of Education, Campbellsville University, and assistant chair, graduate programs.

Traylor, Neely (Ed.D, Eastern Kentucky University). Principal, Bourbon Central Elementary, Paris Independent (Ky.). Served in school support at the Kentucky Department of Education.

Wallace, Joseph "Rocky" (SL.D, Regent University). Professor, graduate education leadership, Campbellsville University.

Watts, Leslie Todd (MA, Morehead State University). Principal, Ewing Elementary, Fleming County (Ky.). Currently working on Ed.D at Morehead State University.

Wilcox, Ben (MA, Eastern Kentucky University). Kentucky State School Security Marshal. Worked for Department of Criminal Justice as instructional design section supervisor.

Young, Lu Settles (Ed.D, Northern Kentucky University). Executive director, Next Generation Academy at the University of Kentucky, and chair of Kentucky School Board.

About the Editors

Rocky Wallace is professor in graduate studies at Campbellsville University. He has helped develop similar graduate education leadership programs at Asbury University and Morehead State University. Rocky is a former teacher, coach, school principal of a U.S. Blue Ribbon School, served in the Highly Skilled Educator school leader support program at the Kentucky Department of Education, and as director of instructional support and adult education at KEDC (education coop in Ashland, Kentucky). This is his twelfth book project with Rowman & Littlefield.

Ann Burns is associate professor and leadership programs coordinator at Eastern Kentucky University (EKU). Ann currently teaches school administration and educational doctoral courses at EKU. Her professional career has spanned all levels of P–12 education and postsecondary, including classroom teacher, school and district administrator, director of education recovery for the Kentucky Department of Education, education cooperative consultant, and university professor.

Stephanie Sullivan is assistant professor at Murray State University, where she has been the coordinator of the education administration program and currently serves as chair of the early childhood and elementary department. Stephanie formerly served in the K–12 setting as a teacher, counselor, and administrator. As principal, she led her school to achieve National Blue Ribbon School status, and she was named 2009 Administrator of the Year by the National Association of Elementary School Principals

www.ingramcontent.com/pod-product-compliance
Lightning Source LLC
Chambersburg PA
CBHW030141240426
43672CB00005B/217